Apple Slices

French Gingerbread Slices

Quick Rusks

Cardamom Meringues

Aja Cookies

Sugar-Free Almond Shells

Italian Anise Biscotti

Rye Logs

Choco-Coco Squares

Christmas Stars

Arrak Rolls

Grandmother's Spritz Wreaths

SWEDISH

CAKES AND COOKIES

SWEDISH
CAKES AND COOKIES

ENGLISH TRANSLATION: MELODY FAVISH

SKYHORSE PUBLISHING

Copyright © 2008 by Skyhorse Publishing, Inc.
Originally published as *Sju Sorters Kakor* © 2005 ICA
bokförlag, Forma Publishing Group AB, Västerås, Sweden.

Skyhorse Publishing books may be purchased in bulk at
special discounts for sales promotion, corporate gifts, fund
raising, or educational purposes. Special editions can also
be created to specifications. For details, contact Special
Sales Department, Skyhorse Publishing, 307 West 36th
Street, 11th Floor, New York, NY 10018 or
info@skyhorsepublishing.com.

www.skyhorsepublishing.com

17 16 15 14 13 12 11 10 9 8

Library of Congress Cataloging-in-Publication Data
Sju sorters kakor. English
  Swedish cakes and cookies / English translation, Melody
Favish.
    p. cm.
  ISBN 978-1-60239-262-5 (hardcover : alk. paper) 1.
Cake. 2. Cookies. 3. Cookery, Swedish. I. Favish,
Melody. II. Title. III. Title: Swedish cakes & cookies.

TX771.S422413 2008
641.8'653—dc22
                    2007049947

Recipes and text: ICA test kitchens
Cover and typography: Typoform
Photos: Studio Ulf Christer, Kent Jardhammar, and
Håkan Flank
Color repro: Scarena
English translation: Melody Favish

Printed in China

Contents

Foreword

The coffee klatch with seven different kinds of cookies is an important institution in Sweden. Our country is also the only place in the world that calls such an informal gathering a party. Many people love to bake sweet breads and cakes, and getting together with friends for coffee and cake is one of life's simple pleasures. But in today's world, there is seldom time for more than one or two kinds of cake.

The story behind the book

This recipe collection has been around for quite a few years. It was first published in 1945, in conjunction with a cake-baking contest. That was right after World War II ended, and we had lived with ration cards for a long time. Cake-baking in the home had been reduced to a minimum. There was enormous interest in the contest, and over 8000 recipes were submitted. That was a lot in those days. The recipes were assembled in a book called "Sju sorters kakor (Seven kinds of cakes)" and it became a best-seller.

The first edition sold out quickly. And over the years, changes were made. Old measurements disappeared, and substitutes for hard-to-get ingredients were no longer necessary. A new baking contest was held in 1965, and that attracted in 16,000 entries, proof that there was still great interest in baking! The contest was divided into seven categories, and the finals were held at ICA Test Kitchens in Stockholm, where 21 "bakers" prepared their best recipes.

Recipes from that competition were collected in a new edition of the book. Public health advisories calling for less fat and sugar in the diet were taken very seriously, and that could be seen in the recipes.

In 1975, it was time for a new contest. Recipes for healthy and low-caloric baked goods were in demand. Baking at home had become more popular, but many people really didn't know how to bake. The next edition of this book focused on the beginning baker. There were basic recipes for different kinds of dough, with information about the ingredients used in baking, as well as series of pictures that showed how to make cakes and pastries step by step. Many recipes from the 1965 edition were included, but often in a new version. Modern ovens and tools demanded meticulous testing. In addition, the use of certain ingredients has changed over the years. For example, today's recipes call for less flour.

Ten years later, in 1985, this book was revised once again. Interest in baking had hardly been satisfied. A picture of every cake was included in this edition. Beginners and everyone else needed to be convinced that baking is both easy and enjoyable. At the beginning of each chapter, there was also practical advice. Recipes that won earlier contests were also given credit in the new book.

After 60 years, Swedes still like to bake cakes and set a festive table, as was written in the foreward to the 1945 edition. Many of the recipes in the newest edition are classics that we can't live without. That's why we have been extra careful with our revisions of this beloved book.

Have fun and happy baking!

The oven

The right place and the right heat

For the best results, you need an oven with a reliable thermostat, so that you can select the correct temperature. Ten degrees Celsius (twenty Fahrenheit) plus or minus does not matter much.

The placement of a cake in the oven is important for the result.

Rolls, pastries, baking-powder breads, muffins, jelly rolls and cookies should be placed in the center of the oven.

Cakes, bar cookies, sweet breads and Danish or puff pastry lengths should be placed in the lower part of the oven.

Baking with a convection oven

In a regular oven, the heat comes from elements at the top and bottom, so it can hold only one baking sheet at a time.

In a convection oven, a fan forces the air around the entire oven. Since the hot air reaches all parts of the oven, several sheets of pastries can be baked at once. It is also possible to bake different things in the oven, as long as they all require the same temperature. They can, however, have different cooking times.

With a convection oven, the temperature should be around 10 percent lower.

Cookies, rolls and muffins should be baked on the center oven shelf.

Mixing, beating and kneading by machine

Mixing, beating and kneading are hard work when done by hand. A mixer can save both time and energy. There are many kinds of machines, including blenders, heavy-duty stand mixers, hand-held electric mixers, and food processors, that are useful additions to the kitchen.

BLENDER

A blender can be purchased on its own or as an attachment to a large multi-purpose kitchen machine. It has a glass or plastic container and rotating blades that chop and blend. It is particularly useful for chopping almonds or other nuts and for pureeing fruit and berries for sauces and cake fillings.

HEAVY-DUTY STAND ELECTRIC MIXER

These machines always have a large bowl, as well as beaters and dough hooks. Although they generally come in two sizes, the smaller one, with a capacity of 5 dl (2 cups) liquid, is usually big enough for most households.

The best machines have a **flat beater** for creaming butter and eggs and mixing cake batter, plus another shaped like a **whisk** for beating egg whites.

Dough hooks can be used to beat butter and sugar for cookies, and they take the work out of kneading yeast dough.

Do not overmix. No dough should be overworked. Most cake batters are best after 3–4 minutes, while 5 minutes is usually enough for sweet yeast breads.

HAND-HELD ELECTRIC MIXER

If you need a machine for beating cake batter or light kneading, a simple electric mixer will accomplish those tasks very well. Check the grip – it should sit well in the hand, and it shouldn't be too heavy. Some mixers come with a stand as well.

For batter and dough. A hand-held mixer is good for beating eggs and sugar for sponge cakes, or beating butter and sugar for pound cakes. Use the beaters for egg whites and cream, otherwise use the dough hooks. Normally, it isn't necessary to change attachments to prepare a batter or dough. Yeast dough that contains up to 5 dl (2 cups) liquid can be mixed with beaters.

Remember, do not beat for too long. After 3–4 minutes, an egg and sugar mixture is usually thick enough. If beaten longer, the egg white protein can break down, and the cake will be heavy and compact.

FOOD PROCESSOR

All food processors come with a rotating metal blade that chops and mixes. A food processor is good for cookie dough and small batches of yeast dough. Place all dry ingredients in the food processor bowl. Butter or margarine should be cubed (3 cm / 1 inch) and added after the dry ingredients.

Yeast doughs are prepared in the same way. Fresh yeast can be crumbled or dry yeast sprinkled over the dry ingredients. Liquid should be added through the feeding tube while the machine is running.

For a **moist cake** containing more than 100 g (3 ounces) of butter, the butter and sugar should be processed first and the eggs added one at a time. Flour is added last.

Practical advice

Eggs can vary in size. Unless otherwise indicated, the eggs used in these recipes should weigh around 60 g (2 ounces) each.

> 1 egg yolk = 1 tablespoon
> 1 egg white = around 2 tablespoons

Fat. Butter and stick margarine can be used in breads, cakes, pastries and fillings. Do not use soft margarine in rolled cookie dough. Diet margarines should not be used in baking at all. Liquid margarine and oil can be used instead of solid fat in yeast breads and some cakes.

Farmer cheese or cottage cheese or quark make yeast breads moist and can partially or completely replace the fat in a recipe.

> Count on 250 g (1 cup) farmer cheese per 5 dl (2 cups) liquid in yeast dough. Add 1–2 dl (⅓–¾ cup) more flour.

Leavening agents. Modern baking powder is double acting, so cake batter can rest without deteriorating. The powder releases only a tiny amount of carbon dioxide (what makes cakes rise) at room temperature. Most is released in the oven.

Baking soda needs an acidic component. Baking powder can be substituted at twice the amount stated.

Hartshorn salt, sometimes called baking ammonia, is best in cookies that are very crisp. Baking powder can be substituted at twice the amount stated.

Measuring syrup and honey. Remove the lid and heat the jar for 1–3 minutes at the lowest setting in the microwave oven, or dip in hot water until the desired amount is liquefied.

Melting gelatin. Soak the gelatin sheets in cold water for around 5 minutes. Melt in a saucepan over low heat or in the microwave oven at the top setting for 30–60 seconds depending upon the number of sheets. Let the gelatin cool slightly before mixing into cream or other cold food to avoid formation of gelatin threads. In the following recipes, 1 sheet of gelatin equals ½ teaspoon powdered gelatin.

Weights and Measures

When preparing the recipes, follow the measurements either in metric or imperial; deciliters or cups (1 cup = 8 fluid ounces = 2 ½ dl). Do not combine the two systems within one recipe.

Well-risen dough makes the best bread

Lukewarm liquid. A baking thermometer is indispensable for making sure that the liquid is not too hot. The optimal temperatures are 37°C (100°F) for fresh yeast and 45°C (110°F) for dry yeast.

Fresh yeast or dry yeast. They complement one another. One advantage to dry yeast is that it keeps for around 9 months. There is a difference in preparation. Fresh yeast should be dissolved in liquid, while dry yeast can be mixed in with the flour.

Measure large amounts of flour in a large measuring cup. Pour the flour loosely into the cup. Do not pack the flour down. In most recipes, the amount of flour is approximate. Begin by adding the minimum amount. Too much flour makes the dough hard and short.

Knead until the dough no longer sticks to the sides of the bowl. Work the dough with a heavy wooden spoon for 7–8 minutes, with a machine for around 4 minutes. The finished dough should be shiny and elastic. Sprinkle with flour and cover with a baking cloth or kitchen towel.

Let rise until doubled. Let the covered dough rise at room temperature in a draft-free place for around 30 minutes. That should be enough time for it to double in size.

Knead the dough until it is smooth and elastic. Punch down the dough. Then turn it out onto a lightly floured baking board or counter top. Knead in the remaining flour with easy, rhythmic motions, until the dough is easy to handle and does not stick to your hands or to the baking board. Use as little flour as possible.

The right amount of rising. Cover the shaped loaves and let them rise in a warm and draft-free place for 20–40 minutes. Keep watch. Check if the dough has risen enough by sticking a finger into it. If the indentation disappears as soon as you remove your finger, the dough is ready.

Brush for color and shine. Egg produces good color and shine. Whisk the egg with a few grains of salt to make it thinner. Brush lightly.

Note for the English edition.
All the yeast bread recipes in this book are made with fresh yeast. Equivalent amounts of dry yeast are given in the ingredient list. Stir the dry yeast into the first amount of flour added and proceed with the recipe as written.

Coconut Horns, page 25

CARDAMOM ROLLS

(basic dough) approx. 45 rolls

- Oven temp: 250°C (450°F), convection 225°C (425°F)

150 g (⅔ cup) stick margarine or butter
5 dl (2 cups) milk
50 g (1¾ ounces) fresh yeast or 2 tablespoons active dry yeast
½ teaspoon salt
1–1½ dl (½ cup) sugar
2 teaspoons ground cardamom
approx. 13 dl (5⅓ cups) all-purpose flour

Filling:
100–125 g (4 ounces) almond paste
2 teaspoons ground cardamom
50 g (3 tablespoons) stick margarine or
  butter

Brushing and garnish:
1 egg, lightly beaten
pearl sugar

▶ Melt the margarine in a saucepan. Add the milk and heat until lukewarm, around 37°C (100°F). If using active dry yeast, heat to 45°C (115°F).

Crumble the yeast in a large bowl and add some of the milk mixture, stirring until dissolved. Add the remaining liquid, salt, sugar, cardamom and around ⅔ of the flour, mixing to combine.

Knead the dough until smooth and elastic. Add more flour, but reserve 1–2 dl (½–¾ cup). The dough is ready when it no longer sticks to the sides of the bowl. Sprinkle a little flour over the dough so that it doesn't dry out. Cover with a cloth and set in a warm, draft-free place. Let rise until doubled.

Punch down the dough and knead it in the bowl for a few minutes. Turn out onto a lightly floured surface. Knead in the remaining flour. The dough is ready when it no longer sticks to the sides of the bowl and hands. If the dough is cut, the exposed surface should have even pores. If there are big holes, it hasn't been kneaded enough.

Grate the almond paste and mix with the cardamom and butter until smooth.

Divide the dough in half. Roll each half into a flat rectangle on a lightly floured surface. Spread the filling over the dough. Roll up and cut into even slices. Place them, cut side up, in paper baking cups or on a parchment-lined baking sheet.

Cover and let rise until doubled. Brush with beaten egg and sprinkle with sugar.

Bake on the center oven rack for 8–10 minutes.

PLAIN ROLLS *approx. 60 rolls*

Oven temp: 250°C (450°F), convection oven 225°C (425°F)

1 batch Cardamom Roll dough
2 dl (¾ cup) raisins (optional)

Brushing:
1 egg, lightly beaten

▶ Prepare the dough according to the recipe for Cardamom Rolls.

Knead the raisins into the dough, if desired. Divide the dough into three equal parts. Cut into 20 pieces of equal size. Roll each piece lightly against the baking board with a cupped hand. Press hard to begin with, more gently as the ball becomes round and smooth. Place on greased or parchment-lined baking sheets.

Cover and let rise until doubled. Brush with beaten egg. Bake on the center oven rack for 8–10 minutes.

CINNAMON SWIRLS *approx. 45 rolls*

■ *Oven temp: 250°C (450°F), convection oven 225°C (425°F)*

1 batch Cardamom Roll dough

Filling:
75–100 g (5–7 tablespoons) stick margarine or butter, softened
1 dl (⅓ cup) sugar
2 teaspoons ground cinnamon

Brushing and garnish:
1 egg, lightly beaten
pearl sugar
chopped almonds

▶ Prepare the dough according to the recipe for Cardamom Rolls.

Divide the dough in half. Roll each half into a flat rectangle on a lightly floured surface. Combine the ingredients for the filling and spread over the dough. Roll up and cut into even slices. Place them, cut side up, in paper baking cups or on parchment-lined baking sheets.

Cover and let rise until doubled. Brush with beaten egg and sprinkle with sugar and almonds.

Bake on the center oven rack for 8–10 minutes.

VEGA ROLLS *approx. 45 rolls*

■ *Oven temp: 250°C (450°F), convection 225°C (425°F)*

1 batch Cardamom Roll dough

Filling:
75–100 g (5–7 tablespoons) stick margarine or butter, softened
1 dl (⅓ cup) sugar
2 teaspoons vanilla sugar or 1 teaspoon vanilla extract

Brushing:
1 egg, lightly beaten

▶ Prepare the dough according to the recipe for Cardamom Rolls.

Divide the dough in three pieces of equal size. Roll each piece into a flat rectangle, around 30 × 50 cm (12 × 20 inches) on a lightly floured surface. Combine the ingredients for the filling and spread over the dough. Roll up and cut into 2–3 cm (1 inch) slices. Press each slice down in the center with the handle of a wooden spoon, so that the ends turn up. Place on greased or parchment-lined baking sheet.

Cover and let rise until doubled. Brush with beaten egg. Bake on the center oven rack for 8–10 minutes.

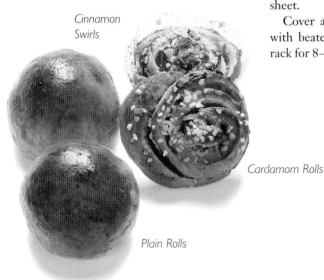

Cinnamon Swirls

Cardamom Rolls

Plain Rolls

SNACK ROLLS *24 buns*

Good, extra protein-rich and not too sweet, these rolls make the perfect between-meal snack.

- *Oven temp: 250°C (450°F), convection 225°C (425°F)*

25 g (2 tablespoons) stick margarine or butter
2½ dl (1 cup) milk
25 g (1 ounce) fresh yeast or 1 tablespoon active dry yeast
½ dl (3 tablespoons) sugar
100 g (½ cup) cottage cheese
approx. 8 dl (3⅓ cups) all-purpose flour
Brushing:
1½ tablespoons milk + 2 teaspoons sugar or 1 egg, lightly beaten

▶ Melt the margarine in a saucepan. Add the milk and heat until lukewarm, around 37°C (100°F). If using active dry yeast, heat to 45°C (115°F).

Crumble the yeast in a large bowl and add some of the milk mixture, stirring until dissolved. Add the remaining liquid, salt, sugar, cottage cheese and around ⅔ of the flour, mixing to combine.

Knead the dough until smooth and elastic. The dough is ready when it no longer sticks to the sides of the bowl. Sprinkle a little flour over the dough so that it doesn't dry out. Cover with a cloth and set in a warm, draft-free place. Let rise until doubled.

Punch down the dough and turn out onto a lightly floured surface. Knead in the remaining flour. Roll into balls. Place on greased or parchment-lined baking sheets.

Cover and let rise until doubled. Brush with milk mixed with sugar or beaten egg. Bake on the center oven rack for 8–10 minutes.

SWEET PRETZELS *16 pretzels*

☆ This recipe won a prize in 1965. The dough needs only one rising.

- *Oven temp: 275°C (475°F), convection 225°C (425°F)*

100 g (7 tablespoons) stick margarine or butter
3 dl (1¼ cups) milk
1 dl (½ cup) sugar
50 g (1¾ ounces) fresh yeast or 2 tablespoons active dry yeast
8½ dl (3½ cups) all-purpose flour
Brushing:
beaten egg (optional)

▶ Melt the margarine in a saucepan. Add the milk and heat until lukewarm, around 37°C (100°F). If using active dry yeast, heat to 45°C (115°F). Pour the milk mixture into a mixer bowl. Add the sugar and yeast, stirring until dissolved. Add half the flour, mixing at high speed. Knead in the remaining flour, working the dough until smooth and elastic. If it sticks to the sides of the bowl, let it rest a few minutes, then turn it out onto a lightly floured surface. It should be quite loose and feel "alive" and warm.

Divide the dough into 16 pieces of equal size. Form each into long strips and twist into pretzels. Place on a greased or parchment-lined baking sheet. Cover and let rise for around 30 minutes

Brush with beaten egg if desired. Bake on the center oven rack for around 5 minutes.

COFFEE ROLLS *approx. 20 rolls*

These rolls are also called Quick Rolls because they are made with baking powder

- *Oven temp: 225°C (425°F), convection 200°C (400°F)*

5 dl (2 cups) all-purpose flour
2½ teaspoons baking powder
¾ teaspoon ground cardamom
100 g (7 tablespoons) stick margarine or butter
1 egg
2 dl (¾ cup) milk
Brushing and garnish:
1 egg, lightly beaten
pearl sugar
chopped almonds

▶ Combine flour, baking powder, sugar and cardamom. Cut the butter into the flour mixture. Add the egg and milk, working quickly to combine.

Spoon into paper baking cups. Brush with beaten egg and sprinkle with sugar and almonds.

Bake on the center oven rack for around 10 minutes.

ALMOND PUCKS *25 pucks*

Cultured buttermilk can be used instead of sour cream, and 4 teaspoons baking powder can be used instead of hornsalt or baking ammonia.

- *Oven temp: 225°C (425°F), convection 200°C (400°F)*

100 g (7 tablespoons) stick margarine or butter, softened
1½ dl (⅔ cup) sugar
1 egg

2 dl (¾ cup) dairy sour cream
2 teaspoons hornsalt (baking ammonia) or 4 teaspoons baking powder
5½ dl (2¼ cups) all-purpose flour
½ teaspoon almond extract
Garnish:
pearl sugar
chopped almonds (optional)

▶ Beat the butter and sugar until light and fluffy. Add the remaining ingredients.

Form the dough into a roll and slice. Place on greased or parchment-lined baking sheets. Pat into lightly rectangular shapes. Sprinkle with sugar and almonds, if desired.

Bake on the center oven rack for around 10 minutes.

FILLED ROLLS *(basic dough) around 20 rolls*

The filling gives these rolls their name. It can be varied in many ways.

2 dl (¾ cup) half and half
25 g (1 ounce) fresh yeast or 1 tablespoon active dry yeast
75 g (5 tablespoons) stick margarine or butter, softened
3 tablespoons sugar
1 egg
approx. 8 dl (3 ⅓ cups) all-purpose flour

▶ Heat the half and half until lukewarm 37 °C (100 °F). If using active dry yeast, heat to 45 °C (115 °F). Crumble the yeast in a little of the liquid.

Beat the butter and sugar until light and fluffy. Add the egg, the dissolved yeast and the remaining liquid. Knead in the flour until smooth and elastic. Cover and let rise until almost doubled.

Proceed according to the following recipes.

VANILLA ROLLS *20 rolls*

■ *Oven temp: 250 °C (450 °F), convection 225 °C (425 °F)*
1 batch Filled Roll dough
Filling:
3 dl (1 ¼ cups) vanilla custard cream or pudding
Brushing and garnish:
melted butter or margarine
sugar

▶ Prepare the dough according to the recipe for Filled Rolls.

Prepare the filling.

Roll the dough into a large rectangle. Cut out rounds with a plain cookie cutter, around 9 cm (3 ¾ inches) in diameter. Top with a spoonful of filling. Pinch together into balls. Place, seam side down, on greased or parchment-lined baking sheets. Let rise until almost doubled.

Bake on the center oven rack for around 10 minutes.

Brush the finished rolls with melted butter and dip in sugar.

APPLE ROLLS *20 rolls*

■ *Oven temp: 250 °C (450 °F), convection 225 °C (425 °F)*
1 batch Filled Roll dough
Filling:
2 dl (1 cup) thick applesauce
1 teaspoon cinnamon
Brushing and garnish:
1 egg, lightly beaten
pearl sugar

▶ Prepare the dough according to the recipe for Filled Rolls.

Combine the applesauce and cinnamon.

Roll the dough into a large rectangle. Cut out rounds with a plain cookie cutter, around 9 cm (3 ¾ inches) in diameter. Top with a spoonful of filling. Pinch together into balls. Place, seam side down, on greased or parchment-lined baking sheets. Let rise until almost doubled.

Brush with beaten egg and sprinkle with pearl sugar. Bake on the center oven rack for around 10 minutes.

ODEN ROLLS *20 buns*

◾ *Oven temp: 250°C (450°F),*
  convection 225°C (425°F)

I batch Filled Roll dough

Filling:
100 g (4 ounces) almond paste
2 teaspoons ground cardamom
2 tablespoons stick margarine or butter

Brushing and garnish:
I egg, lightly beaten
sliced almonds

▶ Prepare the dough according to the recipe for Filled Rolls.

Grate the almond paste and mix with the cardamom and butter.

Roll the dough into a large rectangle. Cut into squares. Top each with a spoonful of filling. Pinch together into small square packets. Place, seam side down, on greased or parchment-lined baking sheets. Let rise until almost doubled.

Brush with beaten egg and sprinkle with almonds. Bake on the center oven rack for around 10 minutes.

CINNAMON BRIOCHES

approx. 30 rolls

◾ *Oven temp: 250°C (450°F),*
  convection 225°C (425°F)

2 dl (¾ cup) milk
50 g (1¾ ounces) fresh yeast or
  2 tablespoons active dry yeast
4 dl (1⅔ cups) all-purpose flour
½ teaspoon salt
150 g (⅔ cup) stick margarine or butter
5 eggs
approx. I liter (4 cups) all purpose flour

Filling:
125 g (½ cup) stick margarine or
  butter, softened
2 dl (¾ cup) sugar
2–3 teaspoons
  cinnamon

Brushing:
I egg, lightly beaten

▶ Heat the milk to 37°C (100°F). If using active dry yeast, heat to 45°C (115°F). Crumble the yeast into the milk, stirring until dissolved. Add the first amount of flour and salt. Knead this "basic dough" until smooth and elastic. Cover and let rise until doubled.

Beat the margarine and sugar. Beat in the eggs, combining well. Add to the dough and gradually knead in the remaining flour. Turn out onto a lightly floured surface and knead until smooth and elastic. Form into smooth balls. Place on a parchment-lined baking sheet. Combine all ingredients in the filling. Lightly flatten the rolls and make a deep hole in the middle of each. Fill with the cinnamon mixture. Let rise until almost doubled.

Brush with beaten egg. Bake on the center oven rack for 8–10 minutes.

LENTEN BUNS *12–15 buns*

- Oven temp: 250°C (450°F),
  convection 225°C (425°F)

100 g (7 tablespoons) stick margarine or
  butter

3 dl (1¼ cups) milk

50 g (1¾ ounces) fresh yeast or 2 tablespoons active dry yeast

½ teaspoon salt

1 dl (⅓ cup) sugar

1 egg

1½ teaspoons baking powder

scant 1 liter (4 cups) all-purpose flour

Brushing:
1 egg, lightly beaten

Filling 1:
150 g (5 ounces) almond paste

Filling 2:
125 g (1 cup) ground almonds
crumbs from inside of buns
1 dl (⅓ cup) hot milk
1 dl (⅓ cup) sugar

Garnish:
2 dl (¾ cup) whipping cream
powdered sugar

▶ Melt the butter and add the milk. Heat to 37°C (100°F). If using active dry yeast, heat to 45°C (115°F).

Crumble the yeast in a large bowl and add salt, sugar, milk mixture and egg. Combine baking powder and flour and add, kneading until smooth and elastic. Cover and let rise for 30 minutes in the bowl.

Turn out onto a lightly floured surface and knead until smooth and elastic. Form into round balls. Place on a greased or parchment-lined baking sheet. Cover and let rise until doubled.

Brush with beaten egg. Bake on the center oven rack for 8–10 minutes.

Let cool.

Cut off the tops of the buns and remove some of the crumbs in the center, but do not break through the outer surface of the buns. Fill with some of the fillings.

Filling 1: Place a little almond paste in each bun. It can be mixed with a little of the cream for garnish, if desired.

Filling 2: Combine all ingredients to a loose filling.

Whip the cream and place a spoonful on top of the filling, or pipe around the filling. Top with the lid. Sift powdered sugar over.

GIANT BUNS *2 buns*

One large bun can be served in wedges like a cake with coffee.

■ *Oven temp: 200°C (400°F),*
   convection 175°C (350°F)

Form the dough into two large buns, around 18 cm (7 inches) in diameter. Bake for 15–20 minutes. Fill according to the above recipe.

COCONUT HORNS *24 rolls*

■ *Oven temp: 250°C (450°F),*
   convection 225°C (425°F)

50 g (1¾ ounces) fresh yeast or 2 tablespoons active dry yeast
150 g (⅔ cup) stick margarine or butter
3 dl (1¼ cups) milk
¾ dl (⅓ cup) sugar
½ teaspoon salt
1 egg
approx. 11 dl (4½ cups) all-purpose flour

Filling:
50 g (3 tablespoons) stick margarine or
   butter
½ dl (¼ cup) grated coconut
1 tablespoon sugar
1 teaspoon ground cinnamon
grated zest of 1 orange

Brushing:
beaten egg

▶ Crumble the yeast in a large bowl. Melt the butter and add the milk. Heat to 37°C (100°F). If using active dry yeast, heat to 45°C (115°F). Pour over the fresh yeast, stirring until dissolved. Add the sugar, salt, egg and most of the flour.

Knead the dough until smooth and elastic with a machine or by hand. Sprinkle a little flour over the dough. Cover and let rise for around 30 minutes.

Prepare the filling. Combine all ingredients until smooth.

Turn the dough out onto a lightly floured surface. Knead with the remaining flour until smooth and elastic.

Coconut Horns

Divide the dough into three equal parts. Roll each into a round cake, 30 cm (12 inches) in diameter. Cut each into 8 triangles.

Place spoonfuls of filling on the wide ends. Roll into crescents. Place on a parchment-lined baking sheet. Cover and let rise for around 30 minutes. Brush with beaten egg.

Bake on the center oven rack for 6–8 minutes.

MECKA'S KARLSBAD ROLLS

12 rolls

- Oven temp: *250 °C (450 °F),*
  convection 225 °C (425 °F)
- 25 g (1 ounce) fresh yeast or 1 tablespoon active dry yeast
- 100 g (7 tablespoons) stick margarine or butter
- 2 ½ dl (1 cup) milk
- 2 tablespoons sugar
- ½ teaspoon salt
- 1 teaspoon hornsalt (baking ammonia) or 2 teaspoons baking powder
- 2 egg yolks
- approx. 8 dl (3 ⅓ cups) all-purpose flour

Filling:
- 350 g (10 ounces) almond paste
- 1–2 egg whites

Brushing and garnish:
- 1 egg, lightly beaten
- sliced almonds

▶ Crumble the yeast in a large bowl. Melt the butter, add the milk and heat to 37 °C (100 °F). If using active dry yeast, heat to 45 °C (115 °F). Pour over the yeast, stirring until dissolved. Add the sugar, salt, hornsalt and egg yolks, beating well. Knead in most of the flour. Knead with a machine or by hand until the dough no longer sticks to the sides of the bowl. Sprinkle with a little flour. Cover and let rise for 30 minutes.

Prepare the filling. Grate the almond paste in a food processor or by hand. Add enough egg white to form a smooth, spreadable mixture.

Turn the dough out onto a lightly floured surface. Knead in the remaining flour. Roll into a 28 × 60 cm (11 × 24 inch) rectangle. Cut into 12 pieces. Place a spoonful of filling in the center of each piece and spread it to cover the center ⅓ of the dough. Fold the sides of dough over the filling to form a 3 cm (1¼ inch) wide roll. Place, seam side down, on a parchment-lined baking sheet. Cover and let rise for around 30 minutes.

Brush with beaten egg and sprinkle with almonds.

Bake on the center oven rack for 6–7 minutes. Remove from the oven, cover and let cool.

KARLSBAD WREATH *one wreath*

Also called Mayor's wreath with filling 2.

- Oven temp: *200 °C (400 °F),*
  convection 175 °C (350 °F)
- 100 g (7 tablespoons) stick margarine or butter
- 2 dl (scant 1 cup) milk
- 25 g (1 ounce) fresh yeast or 1 tablespoon active dry yeast
- pinch salt
- ½–1 dl (⅓ cup) sugar
- 2 egg yolks
- approx. 7 dl (scant 3 cups) all-purpose flour

Filling 1:
- 100 g (4 ounces) almond paste
- 50 g (3 tablespoons) stick margarine or butter

Filling 2:
- 1–2 tablespoons stick margarine or butter
- 1½ dl (⅔ cup) raisins
- 50 g (3 tablespoons) chopped candied orange peel
- 1 dl (⅓ cup) chopped almonds

Brushing:
- 1 egg, lightly beaten

Karlsbad Wreath

▶ Melt the butter. Add the milk and heat to 37 °C (100 °F). If using active dry yeast, heat to 45 °C (115 °F). Crumble the yeast in a large bowl and add a small amount of the liquid, stirring until dissolved. Add the remaining liquid. Knead in the salt, sugar, egg yolks and flour.

Knead until the dough no longer sticks to the sides of the bowl. Sprinkle with a little flour. Cover and let rise until doubled. Turn the dough out onto a lightly floured surface. Roll the dough into a 60 × 25 cm (24 × 10 inch) rectangle. Make filling 1 by combining the almond paste and butter. Spread over the dough. Or use filling 2 and spread the butter over the dough and sprinkle with the remaining ingredients. Leave a 5 cm (2 inch) strip at one end bare. Roll up lengthwise, starting at the filling-covered end. Place, seam side down, on a greased or parchment-lined baking sheet. Make a few slashes in the dough with a sharp knife, if desired. Cover and let rise until almost doubled. Brush with beaten egg. Bake on the lowest oven shelf for 15–20 minutes.

SWEET WREATH *one wreath*

■ *Oven temp: 200 °C (400 °F),*
convection 175 °C (350 °F)

1 ¼ dl (½ cup) half and half
25 g (1 ounce) fresh yeast or 1 tablespoon
active dry yeast
50 g (3 tablespoons) stick margarine or
butter
approx. 5 dl (2 cups) all-purpose flour
pinch salt
2 teaspoons sugar
1 egg
1 teaspoon ground cardamom

Filling:
100 g (7 tablespoons) stick margarine or
butter
¾ dl (⅓ cup) sugar
1 teaspoon ground cardamom

Brushing and garnish:
1 egg, lightly beaten
pearl sugar
chopped almonds

▶ Heat the half and half to 37 °C (100 °F). If
using active dry yeast, heat to 45 °C (115 °F).
Crumble the yeast in a large bowl and add
the liquid, stirring until dissolved.

Cut the butter into most of the flour. Add
the liquid and remaining ingredients. Knead
until smooth and elastic. Cover and let rise
until almost doubled.

Turn the dough out onto a lightly floured
surface. Lightly knead in the remaining
flour.

Roll the dough into a 30 × 50 cm (12 × 20
inches) rectangle.

Beat the butter, sugar and cardamom until smooth. Spread over the dough. Roll up
lengthwise and cut into 10 pieces. Place
them, cut side up, in a greased tube pan,
around 21 cm (9 inches) in diameter. Or cut
the roll into 20 pieces and place them, slightly overlapping, in a 24 cm (10 inch) spring-
form pan. Cover and let rise until doubled,
around 40 minutes.

Brush with beaten egg. Sprinkle with
pearl sugar and almonds. Bake on the lowest
oven shelf for 15–20 minutes. The wreath
can be moved to the middle of the oven toward the end of the baking time.

APPLE WREATH *one wreath*

■ *Oven temp: 200 °C (400 °C),*
convection 175 °C (350 °F)

100 g (7 tablespoons) stick margarine or
butter
2 dl (¾ cup) half and half
25 g (1 ounce) fresh yeast or 1 tablespoon
active dry yeast
pinch salt
3 tablespoons sugar
2 egg yolks
approx. 8 dl (3 cups) all-purpose flour

Sweet Wreath

Apple Wreath

28

Filling:
1½ dl (⅔ cup) applesauce or grated
　apples with a little sugar
2 teaspoons cinnamon

Brushing and garnish:
1 egg, lightly beaten
pearl sugar

▶ Melt the butter in a saucepan. Add the half
and half and heat to 37 °C (100 °F). If using
active dry yeast, heat to 45 °C (115 °F).

Crumble the yeast in a large bowl and add
some of the liquid, stirring until the yeast is
dissolved.

Add the remaining liquid along with the
rest of the ingredients, reserving a little flour
for later. Knead until smooth and elastic.
Cover and let rise for 20–30 minutes.

Turn the dough out onto a lightly floured
surface. Knead for a few minutes. Roll into
a 30 × 50 cm (12 × 20 inch) rectangle. Spread
the applesauce or the grated apples over the
dough. Sprinkle with cinnamon.

Roll up lengthwise. Place, seam side down,
on a greased or parchment-lined baking
sheet. Form into a wreath. Make a few slashes in the dough with a sharp knife. Cover and
let rise until almost doubled, around 40 minutes.

Brush with beaten egg. Sprinkle with
pearl sugar. Bake on a low oven
rack for 20–25 minutes.

QUICK WREATH *one wreath*

■ *Oven temp: 200 °C (400 °F), convection 175 °C
(350 °F)*

6 dl (2½ cups) all-purpose flour
2½ teaspoons baking powder
1 dl (⅓ cup) sugar
100 g (7 tablespoons) stick margarine or but-
　ter
1 egg
2 dl (¾ cup) milk
1 dl (⅓ cup) raisins
½ dl (3 tablespoons) chopped candied
　orange peel

Brushing and garnish:
1 egg, lightly beaten
pearl sugar

▶ Combine the flour, baking powder and
sugar. Cut the butter into the flour mixture.
Whisk egg and milk and add, mixing lightly.
Stir in the fruit. Form the dough into a
wreath on a greased or parchment-lined baking sheet. Brush with lightly beaten egg.
Sprinkle with pearl sugar.

Bake on the center oven rack for 15–20
minutes. Serve on the same day.

Quick Wreath

CARDAMOM LENGTHS *3 or 4 lengths*

- ■ *Oven temp: 200°C (400°F), convection 175°C (350°F)*
- 150 g (⅔ cup) stick margarine or butter
- 5 dl (2 cups) milk
- 50 g (1¾ ounces) fresh yeast or 2 tablespoons active dry yeast
- ½ teaspoon salt
- 1–1½ dl (½ cup) sugar
- 2 teaspoons ground cardamom
- 1 egg
- approx. 15 dl (6¼ cups) all-purpose flour

Brushing and garnish:
- 1 egg, lightly beaten
- pearl sugar, if desired

▶ Melt the butter in a saucepan. Add the milk and heat to 37°C (100°F). If using active dry yeast, heat to 45°C (115°F).

Crumble the yeast in a large bowl and add a little of the milk mixture, stirring until dissolved. Add the remaining ingredients, but only a little over half the flour. Knead the dough until shiny, porous and elastic. Knead in the remaining flour by hand, reserving a little for later. Knead until the dough no longer sticks to the side of the bowl. Sprinkle with flour. Cover and let rise for 30–40 minutes.

Turn the dough out onto a lightly floured surface. Knead until smooth and elastic. Divide into 3 or 4 equal parts. Form into flat lengths. Place on a greased or parchment-lined baking sheet. Cover and let rise until almost doubled.

Brush with beaten egg. Sprinkle with pearl sugar, if desired. Bake on a low oven rack for 15–20 minutes.

BRAIDS *3 braids*

- ■ *Oven temp: 200°C (400°F), convection 175°C (350°F)*
- 1 batch Cardamom Length dough

Brushing and garnish:
- 1 egg, lightly beaten
- pearl sugar, if desired

▶ Prepare the dough according to the recipe for Cardamom Lengths. Divide into 3 equal parts. Knead each part until smooth and elastic. Divide each into 3 or 4 pieces. Roll into smooth, even ropes. Braid them.

Place the braids on a greased or parchment-lined baking sheet. Cover and let rise until almost doubled.

Brush with beaten egg. Sprinkle with pearl sugar, if desired. Bake on a low oven rack for 15–20 minutes.

BRAIDED WREATHS

2 or 3 wreaths

▶ Follow the recipe for Braids, but make longer ropes. Form the braids into wreaths when placing on the baking sheet.

FILLED LENGTHS *3–4 lengths*

■ *Oven temp: 200°C (400°F),*
  convection 175°C (350°F)

1 batch Cardamom Length dough

Cinnamon filling:

100 g (7 tablespoons) stick margarine or butter, softened

¾ dl (⅓ cup) sugar

½–1 tablespoon cinnamon

Almond or other nut filling:

125 g (1 cup) ground or finely chopped almonds or other nuts

100 g (7 tablespoons) stick margarine or butter, softened

1 dl (⅓ cup) sugar

Brushing:

1 egg, lightly beaten

▶ Prepare the dough according to the recipe for Cardamom Lengths. Divide into 3–4 equal parts. Roll each into a 20 × 35 cm (8 × 14 inch) rectangle.

Prepare the filling.

Cinnamon filling: Combine all ingredients, mixing well.

Almond or other nut filling: Combine all ingredients, mixing well.

Spread the filling over the dough. Roll up horizontally. Place, seam side down, on a greased or parchment-lined baking sheet. Slice ¾ through at 3 cm (1¼ inch) intervals. Press one slice to the left, one to the right, alternating for the entire length of the dough. Cover and let rise until almost doubled. Brush with beaten egg. Bake on a low oven rack for 15–20 minutes.

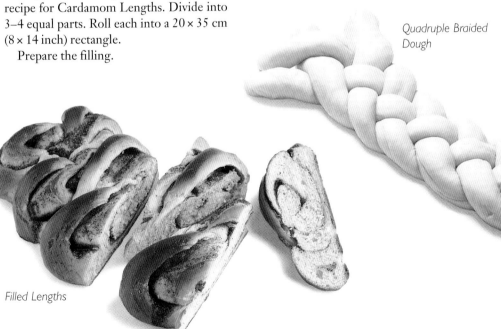

Quadruple Braided Dough

Filled Lengths

STREUSEL CAKE *one cake*

- Oven temp: 225°C (425°F),
  convection 200°C (400°F)
1 dl (½ cup) milk
2 tablespoons stick margarine or butter
25 g (1 ounce) fresh yeast or 1 tablespoon
   active dry yeast
3½ dl (1½ cups) all-purpose flour
pinch salt
2 teaspoons sugar
½ egg

Brushing and garnish:
½ dl (¼ cup) all-purpose flour
½ dl (¼ cup) sugar
½ dl (¼ cup) chopped almonds
2 tablespoons stick margarine or butter
½ egg, lightly beaten

▶ Heat the milk and butter to 37°C (100°F).
If using active dry yeast, heat to 45°C
(115°F). Crumble in the yeast, stirring until
dissolved. Place around half the flour in a
large bowl. Add the yeast mixture, salt, sugar
and egg. Knead until smooth and elastic. Add
the remaining flour, reserving a little for later. Cover and let rise for around 1 hour.

Turn the dough out onto a lightly floured
surface. Knead lightly and form into a round,
smooth cake, around 22 cm (9 inches) in diameter. Place on a greased or parchment-
lined baking sheet. Cover and let rise until
doubled, around 30 minutes at room temperature.

Combine flour, sugar, almonds and butter.
Brush the cake with beaten egg. Sprinkle
with streusel mixture. Bake on the center
oven rack for 12–15 minutes.

WINDSOR CAKE *one cake*

- Oven temp: 225°C (425°F),
  convection: 200°C (400°F)
1 batch Streusel Cake dough
Filling:
1½ dl (⅔ cup) milk
2¼ teaspoons potato starch or cornstarch
2 teaspoons sugar
1 egg yolk
2–3 teaspoons vanilla sugar or 1 teaspoon
   vanilla extract
100 g (7 tablespoons) stick margarine or butter, softened
2 tablespoons powdered sugar

▶ Bake the Streusel Cake according to the
previous recipe. Let cool completely. Divide
horizontally.

Combine milk, potato starch, sugar and
egg yolk in a saucepan. Heat, stirring fre-
quently, until thickened. Let cool. Stir in the
vanilla.

Beat the butter and sugar. Add the cold
vanilla cream by the tablespoonful. Beat at
high speed to make a light, frothy cream.

Spread over the lower layer, then top with
the streusel layer. Refrigerate for at least one
hour before serving.

Streusel Cake

Windsor Cake

BRAIDED SWEET BREAD *one cake*

Instead of making a separate filling, you can add the filling ingredients to the dough.

- ■ *Oven temp: 200°C (400°F), convection 175°C (350°F)*

1½ dl (⅔ cup) milk
25 g (1 ounce) fresh yeast or 1 tablespoon active dry yeast
grated zest of ½–1 orange
1 dl (⅓ cup) orange juice
1 dl (½ cup) creamed cottage cheese, sieved, or quark
1 dl (½ cup) sugar
1 egg (reserve a little for brushing)
7–8 dl (approx. 3 cups) all-purpose flour

Brushing and garnish:
beaten egg
2 dl (¾ cup) powdered sugar
2–3 tablespoons orange juice

▶ Heat the milk to 37°C (100°F). If using active dry yeast, heat to 45°C (115°F). Crumble the yeast in a large bowl and add the milk, stir-ring until the yeast is dissolved. Add the orange zest and juice, cottage cheese and sugar.

Beat the egg and add most to the dough liquid, reserving the rest for brushing.

Knead in most of the flour. The dough should be smooth but not to stiff. Cover and let rise for around 30 minutes.

Turn the dough out onto a lightly floured surface. Knead with the remaining flour until smooth and elastic.

Divide the dough into 3 equal parts. Roll each piece into a 40 cm (16 inch) long rope. Braid the ropes into a long tight braid.

Form the dough into a round loaf on a greased or parchment-lined baking sheet. Cover and let rise for around 30 minutes. Brush with the remaining egg.

Bake on the center oven rack for 20–25 minutes. Remove from the oven and place on a rack. Cover and let cool. Stir the powdered sugar into the juice. Drizzle over the loaf.

CARDAMOM CAKE *one cake*

- Oven temp: 175°C (350°F),
  convection 150°C (300°F)

200 g (1 scant cup) stick margarine or
  butter
2 eggs
3 dl (1¼ cups) sugar
8 dl (3⅓ cups) all-purpose flour
1 tablespoon baking powder
2½ teaspoons ground cardamom
3 dl (1¼ cups) milk

Garnish:
3–4 tablespoons pearl sugar
coarsely chopped almonds

▶ Grease and flour a 26 cm (10 inch) round cake pan.

Melt the butter and let cool.

Beat eggs and sugar until light yellow and very thick. Add the flour, baking powder, cardamom, milk and melted butter, mixing until combined.

Pour into the prepared pan. Sprinkle with pearl sugar and almonds.

Bake on a low oven rack for around 1 hour. Remove from the pan and cool completely.

Variation: Pour the batter into a greased and floured 30 × 40 (12 by 16 inch) pan. Bake for around 25 minutes. Cool completely. Cut into 40 squares.

FESTIVE GIANT SWEET PRETZEL *2 pretzels*

- Oven temp: 225°C (425°F),
  convection 200°C (400°F)

25 g (1 ounce) fresh yeast or 1 tablespoon
  active dry yeast
2 dl (¾ cup) cold milk
2 tablespoons sugar
150 g (⅔ cup) stick margarine or butter, softened
approx. 6 dl (2⅓ cups) all-purpose flour

Filling:
150 g (⅔ cup) stick margarine or butter
1 dl (½ cup) sugar
3–4 teaspoons vanilla sugar or 2 teaspoons
  vanilla extract

Brushing and garnish:
1 egg, lightly beaten
sugar

▶ Crumble the fresh yeast in a large bowl and add the milk, stirring until the yeast is dissolved. Add sugar, butter and most of the flour. Knead until smooth and elastic.

Turn the dough out onto a lightly floured surface. Knead in the remaining flour. Divide the dough in half. Roll each piece into a 15 × 90 cm (6 × 36 inch) sheet.

Combine ingredients for the filling. Spread over the dough, thick in the middle, thin toward the edges.

Roll each long side toward the middle, leaving around ½ cm (¼ inch) of space between the two rolls. They should not touch. Form the lengths into pretzels on parchment-lined baking sheets.

Let rise, uncovered, at room temperature for around 2 hours. Brush with beaten egg and sprinkle with sugar.

Bake on a low oven rack for around 10 minutes. Let cool slightly, then transfer to a rack.

Pictured on page 15.

HANNELORE'S PAN ROLLS
24 rolls

- *Oven temp: 200 °C (400 °F), convection 175 °C (350 °F)*

Approx. 8 dl (3 ⅓ cups) all-purpose flour
¾ dl (⅓ cup) sugar
½ teaspoon salt
50 g (3 tablespoons) stick margarine or butter
grated zest of 1 lemon
2 ½ dl (1 cup) milk
50 g (1 ¾ ounces) fresh yeast or 2 tablespoons active dry yeast
1 egg

Filling:
24 pitted prunes
100 g (4 ounces) almond paste

Brushing and garnish:
2 tablespoons stick margarine or butter
powdered sugar

▶ Combine most of the flour (reserve 1 dl / ½ cup), sugar and salt in a large bowl. Cut in the butter with an electric mixer or by hand. Add the lemon zest.

Heat the milk to 37 °C (100 °F). If using active dry yeast, heat to 45 °C (115 °F). Crumble in the yeast, stirring until dissolved. Pour over the flour mixture and add the egg. Knead until smooth and elastic. The dough should not stick to the sides of the bowl. Sprinkle with a little flour. Cover and let rise for around 45 minutes.

Stuff each prune with a little chunk of almond paste.

Turn the dough out onto a lightly floured surface. Knead in the remaining flour. Form into a narrow rope. Divide into 24 pieces. Roll each into a round ball. Press one almond paste-filled prune into each, making sure that they are covered completely with dough.

Grease a 20 × 30 cm (8 × 12 inch) pan. Melt the butter, brush or dip the bottom half of the balls in the butter. That makes them easy to pull apart after baking. Place them close together in the pan.

Let rise for around 30 minutes. Brush with more butter, if desired.

Bake on a low oven rack for around 25 minutes. Let cool in the pan. Just before serving, sift over a little powdered sugar.

GRANDMOTHER'S SAFFRON ROLLS *45 rolls*

- Oven temp: *250°C (450°F),*
  convection 200°C (400°F)

50 g (3 tablespoons) stick margarine or butter

5 dl (2 cups) milk

50 g (1¾ ounces) fresh yeast or 2 tablespoons active dry yeast

1 teaspoon salt

2 teaspoons sugar

15 dl (6¼ cups) all-purpose flour

1 gram (⅛ teaspoon) saffron

1 sugar cube or 1 teaspoon cognac

125 g (½ cup) stick margarine or butter, softened

1½ dl (⅔ cup) sugar

1 egg

Brushing and garnish:

1 egg, lightly beaten

raisins

pearl sugar, if desired

▶ Melt the butter in a saucepan. Add the milk and heat to 37°C (100°F). If using active dry yeast, heat to 45°C (115°F). Crumble the yeast in a large bowl and add some of the milk, stirring until dissolved. Add the remaining liquid, salt, sugar and most of the flour. Knead until the dough no longer sticks to the sides of the bowl. Sprinkle with a little flour, cover and let rise until doubled, around 1 hour.

Crush the saffron with the sugar cube in a mortar or mix with the cognac.

Beat the butter and sugar until light and fluffy. Add the saffron and the egg. Knead this mixture into the dough. Add the remaining flour, reserving a little for later. Form into shapes, as pictured. Place on a greased or parchment-lined baking sheet. Cover and let rise until almost doubled.

Brush with beaten egg and garnish with raisins and pearl sugar. Bake on the center oven rack for 8–10 minutes.

Uppland Christmas Cake

SAFFRON BRAIDS *3 braids*

▶ The above dough can be braided. Shaping and baking, see pages 30–31.

UPPLAND CHRISTMAS CAKE

2 cakes

■ *Oven temp: 225 °C (425 °F), convection 200 °C (400 °F)*

1 batch Grandmother's Saffron Roll dough

▶ Prepare the dough and divide in half.

Divide each half into eight 30 cm (12 inch) long, finger-thick ropes. Make a curl on both ends of 7 lengths. Place them cross-wise over one another to form a large pin-wheel, as illustrated on page 36. Roll up the last length and place it on top.

Let rise until almost doubled.

Brush with beaten egg. Bake on a low oven rack for 15–20 minutes.

SAFFRON COTTAGE CHEESE ROLLS *35 rolls*

■ *Oven temp: 225 °C (425 °F), convection 200 °C (400 °F)*

100 g (7 tablespoons) stick margarine or butter
5 dl (2 cups) milk
50 g (1 ¾ ounces) fresh yeast or 2 table-spoons active dry yeast
250 g (1 cup) creamed cottage cheese, sieved, or quark
1 gram (⅛ teaspoon) saffron
1 ½ dl (⅔ cup) sugar
½ teaspoon salt
approx. 16 dl (6 ⅔ cups) all-purpose flour
Brushing:
1 egg, lightly beaten

▶ Melt the butter in a saucepan. Add the milk and heat to 37 °C (100 °F). If using active dry yeast, heat to 45 °C (115 °F).

Crumble the yeast in a large bowl and add the milk mixture, stirring until the yeast is dissolved.

Add the cheese, saffron, sugar, salt and most of the flour. Knead until the dough is smooth and elastic. Cover and let rise for around 40 minutes.

Turn out onto a lightly floured surface. Knead until smooth and elastic. Form into 35 round balls. Arrange them close together in a 30 × 40 cm (12 × 16 inch) pan. Cover and let rise for around 40 minutes.

Brush with beaten egg. Bake on a low oven rack for around 20 minutes.

Cool slightly, then remove from the pan. Cover and cool completely.

Saffron Cottage Cheese Rolls

GLUTEN-FREE WREATH

one wreath

Here is a lovely wreath for those who do not tolerate wheat flour.

- ■ *Oven temp: 200°C (400°F), convection 175°C (350°F)*
- 50 g (3 tablespoons) stick margarine or butter
- 2½ dl (1 cup) milk
- 1 egg yolk
- 25 g (1 ounce) fresh yeast or 1 tablespoon active dry yeast
- ½ dl (3 tablespoons) sugar
- pinch salt
- 1 teaspoon ground cardamom
- approx. 8 dl (3⅓ cups) glutenfree flour mix

Filling:
- 100 g (4 ounces) almond paste
- 1 egg white
- 1 drop green food coloring

Brushing and garnish:
- 1 egg, lightly beaten
- pearl sugar

▶ Melt the butter in a saucepan. Add the milk and heat to 37°C (100°F). If using active dry yeast, heat to 45°C (115°F). Crumble the yeast in a large bowl and add the milk mixture, stirring until the yeast is dissolved.

Add the egg yolk, sugar, salt, cardamom and most of the flour.

Knead until smooth and elastic. Gluten-free dough needs extra long kneading time. Cover and let rise for around 30 minutes.

Mix almond paste, egg white and food coloring in a food processor, or grate the almond paste and mix in the remaining ingredients with a fork.

Turn the dough out onto a lightly floured surface. Knead until smooth and elastic with a little flour. Roll the dough into a 30 × 40 cm (12 × 16 inch) rectangle. Spread with the filling. Roll up lengthwise like a jelly roll. Form into a wreath on a parchment-lined baking sheet.

Slice ¾ through at 3 cm (1¼ inch) intervals. Press one slice to the left, one to the center and one to the right for the entire length of the dough. Cover and let rise for around 30 minutes.

Brush with beaten egg and sprinkle with pearl sugar. Bake on a low oven rack for 20–25 minutes. Remove from the oven, cover and let cool completely.

Gluten-free bread dries out very quickly, so it is a good idea to freeze whatever is not consumed immediately.

Short Long Rusks, page 41, top; Quick Rusks, page 42, center; Italian Anise Biscotti, page 43, bottom.

Rusks ▸

How to make good, crispy rusks.

Brush between the lengths. Make sure there are no cracks in the lengths. Place them close together on a greased baking sheet. Brush with melted butter or oil between the lengths before rising to make them easier to separate after baking.

Halve the rusks horizontally with a serrated knife. The lengths should be cooled completely. Cut all the way through with a serrated knife. Then cut each length crosswise into 2–3 cm (1 inch) wide pieces.

Halve the rusks with a fork for a porous exterior. If you halve the cold rusk rolls with a fork, the exterior will be light and porous.

The oven can be filled with rusks for drying.

4 Toast and dry the rusks.

Toast the rusks, cut surface up, on a baking sheet or in a pan. Place them in a 250°C (450°F) oven and bake until golden.

Dry the rusks in a slow oven, or even after the oven has been turned off. Fill the oven (standard or convection oven) with the toasted rusks. Dry with the door slightly open until they are light and crispy.

Good advice
Be "stingy" with flour in rusks made with yeast. Do not use more flour than absolutely necessary for an elastic, easy to shape dough.

SHORT LONG RUSKS

approx. 100 rusks

- Oven temp: 225°C (425°F),
  convection 200°C (400°F)

150 g (⅔ cup) stick margarine or butter
5 dl (2 cups) milk
50 g (1¾ ounce) yeast or 2 tablespoons
   active dry yeast
½ teaspoon salt
1½ dl (⅔ cup) sugar
1 tablespoon ground cardamom
approx 15 dl (6¼ cups) all-purpose flour

▶ Melt the butter and add the milk. Heat to 37°C (100°F). If using dry yeast, heat to 45°C (115°F).

Crumble the yeast in a large bowl and add some of the milk mixture, stirring until dissolved. Add the remaining liquid, salt, sugar and cardamom. Knead in enough flour to make an elastic dough that does not stick to the sides of the bowl. Sprinkle with a little flour. Cover and let rise for around 30 minutes.

Turn the dough out onto a lightly floured surface. Knead until smooth and elastic with the remaining flour. The dough should be quite loose and rather greasy. Divide the dough into four pieces of equal size. Form each into 40 cm (16 inch) long crack-free ropes.

Place on greased or parchment-lined baking sheets. Cover and let rise for 30–40 minutes.

Bake on the center oven rack for 15–20 minutes. Cool completely.

Halve lengthwise. Cut crosswise into 3 cm (1¼ inch) slices. Toast and dry, see page 40.

DUTCH RUSKS *approx. 100 rusks*

Light, airy rusks

- Oven temp: 250°C (450°F),
  convection 225°C (425°F)

200 g (1 scant cup) butter
2½ dl (1 cup) whipping cream
2½ dl (1 cup) water
75 g (2¾ ounces) fresh yeast or 3 tablespoons active dry yeast
3 eggs
1½ dl (⅔ cup) sugar-
   pinch salt
approx. 16 dl (6⅔ cups)
   all-purpose
   flour

▶ Melt half the butter. Add cream and water and heat to 37°C (100°F). If using dry yeast, heat to 45°C (115°F).

Crumble the yeast in a large bowl and add some of the cream mixture, stirring until dissolved. Add the remaining liquid, eggs, sugar, salt and just over half the flour. Knead until smooth and elastic. Cover and let rise until almost doubled.

Knead in the remaining butter and flour. Roll out to a 1 cm (⅜ inch) thick sheet.

Cut out rounds with a plain cookie cutter, 8–9 cm (3 inches) in diameter. Place them on greased or parchment-lined baking sheets. Let rise, then press down slightly to even them out. Let rise one more time.

Bake on the center oven rack for 5–8 minutes, in a convection oven for 8–10 minutes.

Let cool. Halve crosswise. Toast and dry, see page 40.

QUICK RUSKS *approx. 180 rusks*

These small round rusks are also called Princess Rusks.

■ *Oven temp: 225 °C (425 °F), convection 175 °C (350 °F)*

7 dl (scant 3 cups) all-purpose flour
1½ dl (⅔ cup) sugar
1 tablespoon baking powder
1 teaspoon ground cardamom
150 g (⅔ cup) stick margarine or butter
1½ dl (⅔ cup) milk or cream

▶ Combine the flour (save a little for the final step), sugar, baking powder and cardamom in a large bowl. Cut in the butter. Add the liquid and combine quickly to form a light dough. Turn out onto a lightly floured surface and form small round balls. Place on greased or parchment-lined baking sheets.

Bake on the center oven rack for 8 minutes. Halve with a fork while still warm, and toast lightly in the center of a 150 °C (300 °F) oven until golden and dry.

CARAWAY RUSKS *approx. 250 rusks*

☆ This recipe won a prize in 1984.

■ *Oven temp: 200 °C (400 °F), convection 175 °C (350 °F)*

50 g (1¾ ounces) fresh yeast or 2 tablespoons active dry yeast
100 g (7 tablespoons) stick margarine or butter
2½ dl (1 cup) milk
¼ teaspoon salt
2½ tablespoons caraway seeds
1¾ dl (¾ cup) sugar
8½ dl (3½ cups) all-purpose flour

▶ Crumble the yeast in a large bowl. Melt the butter, add the milk and heat to 37 °C (100 °F). If using dry yeast, heat to 45 °C (115 °F). Pour over the yeast, stirring until dissolved.

Add salt, caraway seed, sugar and most of the flour. Knead until the dough no longer sticks to the bowl. Cover and let rise for 20 minutes.

Turn out onto a lightly floured surface and knead in the remaining flour. The dough should be soft and smooth, but not sticky.

Divide the dough in half, and divide each half into 6 pieces. Using a light hand, roll each piece into a loaf as long as a baking sheet. Place on greased or parchment-lined baking sheets. Cover and let rise for around 40 minutes.

Bake on the center oven rack for around 10

minutes. These should turn only a very light brown. Cover and cool on a rack.

Halve each loaf lengthwise and cut each half crosswise into 1 ½ cm (⅝ inch) pieces.

Place the rusks, cut side up, on baking sheets. Toast one sheet at a time in a 250 °C (450 °F) oven until golden brown. Check often, as they burn easily.

Dry the rusks in a 50–100 °C (120–210 °F) oven for around one hour. All rusks can be dried at the same time with the door slightly open. They can also be dried overnight. Heat the oven, place the rusks inside, then turn off the heat. Let the door stay slightly open.

Form two 30 cm (12 inches) long loaves. Place on a greased or parchment-lined baking sheet.

Bake on the center oven rack for around 25 minutes. Cool on the baking sheet. Cut into 1 cm (⅜ inch) slices.

Place on a baking sheet, cut side up. Toast in a 200 °C (400 °F) oven for around 5 minutes, until golden. Turn and repeat.

Store the biscotti in a tin. If you like a chewy texture, place a piece of fresh bread in the tin.

ITALIAN ANISE BISCOTTI
approx. 35 biscotti

A crispy little rusk that is good with dessert wine, coffee or tea.

- Oven temp: 175 °C (350 °F), convection 175 °C (350 °F)

75 g (5 tablespoons) stick margarine or butter, softened
1 dl (⅓ cup) sugar
2 eggs
1 ¼ dl (½ cup) ground almonds
1 ½ teaspoons ground anise
¼ teaspoon salt
1 ½ teaspoons baking powder
4 dl (1 ⅔ cups) all-purpose flour

▶ Beat the butter and sugar until light and fluffy. Add the eggs, one at a time, beating until light and fluffy. Add the almonds and anise. Combine the dry ingredients and add. Turn the dough out onto a lightly floured surface and knead until smooth.

Italian Anise Biscotti

BERLIN RUSKS *approx. 45 rusks*

Also called Berlin Bread and Almond Rusks.

- *Oven temp: 200°C (400°F), convection 175°C (350°F)*

100 g (7 tablespoons) butter, softened
1 dl (½ cup) sugar
2 eggs
100 g (1 cup) ground almonds
1 teaspoon baking powder
3½ dl (1½ cups) all-purpose flour

▶ Beat the butter and sugar until light and fluffy. Add the eggs, one at a time, beating until light and fluffy. Add the remaining ingredients, mixing well. Form three 30 cm (12 inch) long loaves. Place on a greased or parchment-lined baking sheet.

Bake on the center oven rack for 10–15 minutes. Cool on the baking sheet. Cut into 2 cm (¾ inch) slices. Turn off the oven. Return the rusks to the oven to cool.

MARGARETA'S SPICY RUSKS
approx. 100 rusks

☆ This recipe won a prize in 1945.

- *Oven temp: 200°C (400°F), convection 175°C (350°F)*

125 g (½ cup) stick margarine or butter, softened
2½ dl (1 cup) sugar
1 dl (½ cup) corn syrup
1 egg
125 g (¾ cup) raisins, chopped almonds or finely chopped candied orange peel
2 teaspoons baking soda
6½–7 dl (2¾ cups) all-purpose flour

▶ Beat the butter and sugar until light and fluffy. Add the syrup and egg, beating well. Combine the soda and flour and add. Fold in the fruit. Roll the dough into 8 lengths. Place on a greased or parchment-lined baking sheet.

Bake on the center oven rack for around 15 minutes.

Cut the rusks into 2½ cm (1 inch) wide diagonal slices directly on the baking sheet while still warm.

Envelopes, top; Combs, center; and Twists, bottom. All recipes on page 48.

Danish Pastry ▶

Cold dough makes the best Danish pastry

1 Ingredients right out of the refrigerator. Danish pastry dough should be as cool as possible. Chill the milk, eggs and flour. Mix the yeast and milk together. Add the eggs, sugar, salt and flour. Refrigerate the finished dough for around 10 minutes.

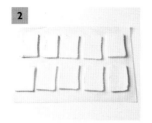

Margarine is better than butter. It is easier to achieve a flaky consistency with solid baking margarine than with butter. Cut cold (right out of the refrigerator) margarine into thin, even slices. Place them on parchment paper for a couple of minutes. If the margarine is too cold and hard, it will be difficult to roll into the dough.

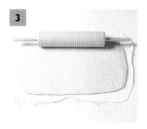

Work in a cool kitchen. Roll the dough out on a lightly floured surface to a 30 × 40 (12 × 16 inch) sheet. Use a good rolling pin. Do not press down the dough too much. Use a light hand.

Roll in the fat. Place margarine slices on half the dough, leaving a 2–3 cm (1 inch) uncovered edge. Fold that edge up against the margarine. Fold the plain dough over the margarine-covered half. Pinch the edges.

5 Roll carefully. Turn the dough by one quarter (If the top points to 12 o'clock, turn it to 3 o'clock). The closed side should be facing you. Roll the dough carefully one more time on the lightly floured surface. Use the rolling pin lightly and roll in only two directions – straight ahead and at a right angle to the side. Do not press down too hard or the dough will split and the margarine won't be rolled in correctly.

Fold the dough into thirds. Brush off loose flour and fold the dough into thirds (like a business letter). Turn the dough by one quarter.

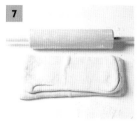

7

Roll out one more time. Roll out the dough, still on a lightly floured surface, until it is around 1 cm (⅜ inch) thick. Brush off any loose flour. Fold into thirds. Turn the dough by one quarter and roll out until it is around 1 cm (⅜ inch) thick. Fold the dough into thirds. Wrap in plastic and refrigerate for 10 minutes.

8

Shape the pastries. Roll the dough one more time until it is around 1 cm (⅜ inch) thick. Divide in half. Wrap each half separately in plastic and refrigerate for 15 minutes.

Roll each half into a rectangular sheet and shape into pastries according to the individual recipes.

DANISH PASTRIES *(basic dough)*

300 g (10 ounces) hard margarine
50 g (1 ¾ ounces) fresh yeast or 2 table-
    spoons active dry yeast
2 ½ dl (1 cup) cold milk
1 egg
½ teaspoon salt
2 tablespoons sugar
approx. 8 dl (3 ⅓ cups) all-purpose flour
Brushing and garnish:
1 egg, lightly beaten
pearl sugar, if desired
chopped almonds or other nuts, if desired

▶ Remove the margarine from the refrigerator and cut into 10 slices. Place on parchment paper or plastic and let sit at room temperature.

Crumble the yeast in a large bowl. Add the milk, stirring until dissolved. Add the egg, salt, sugar and most of the flour, reserving the rest for later. Knead the dough lightly. Wrap in plastic and refrigerate for 10 minutes.

Roll the dough on a lightly floured surface into a 30 × 40 cm (12 × 16 inch) sheet.

Place the margarine slices on half of the dough, leaving a 2–3 cm (1 inch) edge. Fold that edge up against the margarine. Fold the plain dough over the margarine-covered half. Pinch the edges.

Sprinkle the work surface with flour. Turn the dough by one quarter. The closed side should be facing you. Roll the dough out carefully one more time on the lightly floured surface. Do not press down too hard or roll for too long, or the pastry will be flat and hard.

Fold the dough into thirds lengthwise. Turn the dough by one quarter.

Roll out the dough, still on a lightly floured surface, until it is around 1 cm (⅜ inch) thick. The closed side should be facing you. Fold into thirds one more time. Wrap in plastic and refrigerate for 10–15 minutes.

Roll out the dough to a 1 cm (⅜ inch) thick sheet. Divide in half. Wrap each half separately in plastic and refrigerate for 15 minutes.

Prepare pastries from only one half of the dough at a time. The other half should remain in the refrigerator.

ENVELOPES *Approx. 32 pastries*

■ *Oven temp: 250°C (450°F),
   convection 225°C (425°F)*

1 batch Danish Pastry dough, page 47

Almond filling:
150 g (5 ounces) almond paste
½ egg white

Vanilla cream:
2 tablespoons all-purpose flour
1 tablespoon sugar
2½ dl (1 cup) milk
1 egg
2 teaspoons vanilla sugar or 1 teaspoon
   vanilla extract

Brushing and garnish:
egg white or egg
1 dl (⅓ cup) powdered sugar
2 teaspoons water

▶ Prepare the dough according to the recipe for Danish Pastry.

Make the fillings. Grate the almond paste and beat with a small amount of egg white until smooth.

Combine the flour and sugar in a saucepan. Whisk in a little milk, then gradually add the remaining milk and egg. Heat to boiling, stirring constantly. Remove from the heat and let cool. Stir in the vanilla.

Roll both pieces of dough into 36 cm (14 inch) squares. Divide each into 16 pieces. Place a spoonful of almond mixture in the center of each. Fold the corners in to the center and press down. Top with a spoonful of vanilla cream. Let rise.

Bake on the center oven rack for 7–10 minutes. Let cool. Combine powdered sugar and water and drizzle over the pastries. Pictured on page 45.

PASTRY TWISTS *approx. 35 pastries*

■ *Oven temp: 250°C (450°F),
   convection 225°C (425°F)*

1 batch Danish Pastry dough, page 47
   Filling: 1 batch Vanilla cream, see recipe for
   Envelopes

Brushing and garnish: 1 egg white
2 dl (¾ cup) powdered sugar
1½–2 tablespoons water
thinly sliced almonds or other nuts, if desired

▶ Prepare the dough according to the recipe for Danish Pastry. Do not divide. Roll out the dough into a rather thick square. Cut into thin strips and twist one or two strips together. Form into pretzels, knots or figure eights. Place on greased or parchment-lined baking sheets.

Let rise for 1–1½ hours in a cool place.

Place a little vanilla cream in the center of each pastry, if desired. Brush with egg white.

Bake on the center oven rack until golden, 7–10 minutes. Let cool. Combine powdered sugar and water and drizzle over the pastries. Garnish with toasted nuts, if desired. Pictured on page 45.

COMBS *approx. 35 pastries*

■ *Oven temp: 250°C (450°F),
   convection 225°C (425°F)*

1 batch Danish Pastry dough, page 47
Filling:
150 g (5 ounces) almond paste
water or egg white
Brushing and garnish:
1 egg white
pearl sugar
chopped almonds

▶ Prepare the dough according to the recipe for Danish Pastry.

For the filling, grate the almond paste and beat with a small amount of water or egg white until smooth.

Roll out each piece of dough into a 24 × 30 cm (10 × 12 inch) sheet. Spread the filling along the middle of the dough. Fold the sides over the filling. Turn the lengths over, so that the seam is against the baking sheet. Cut across into 4 cm (1¼ inch) pieces. Brush with egg white and dip in a mixture of pearl sugar and almonds.

Place on a greased or parchment-lined baking sheet. Make cuts in the long sides of the pastries. Bend to curve lightly and open the cuts. Let rise for 1–1 ½ hours.

Bake on the center oven rack for 5–8 minutes. Pictured on page 45.

MAYOR'S WREATH *2 wreaths*

■ *Oven temp: 225 °C (425 °F),*
convection 200 °C (400 °F)
1 batch Danish Pastry dough, page 47
Filling:
150 g (5 ounces) almond paste
½–1 egg white
Brushing: egg white

▶ Prepare the dough according to the recipe for Danish Pastry.

Grate the almond paste and beat with a small amount of egg white until smooth. It should not be too loose.

Roll out each piece of dough into a 20 × 50 cm (8 × 20 inch) sheet.

Spread the filling along the middle of the dough. Fold into thirds. Cut into thirds lengthwise, but do not cut completely apart. They should stay joined together at the top. Braid loosely and form into wreaths. Place on greased or parchment-lined baking sheets. Place a small glass in the center, so the wreath keeps its shape. Let rise. Brush with egg white.

Bake on the center oven rack for around 20 minutes.

SIMPLE DANISH PASTRIES
20 pastries
■ *Oven temp: 250 °C (450 °F),*
convection 225 °C (425 °F)
6 dl (2 ½ cups) all-purpose flour
2 tablespoons sugar
100 g (7 tablespoons) stick margarine or butter
50 g (1 ¾ ounces) fresh yeast or 2 tablespoons active dry yeast
¾ dl (⅓ cup) cold half and half
2 eggs
Filling:
100 g (7 tablespoons) stick margarine or butter, softened
½–1 dl (⅓ cup) powdered sugar
4 teaspoons ground cardamom or
1 teaspoon vanilla extract
Brushing and garnish:
1 egg, lightly beaten
sliced almonds

▶ Combine the flour and sugar. Cut in the butter. Crumble the yeast into the half and half, stirring until dissolved. Pour over the flour mixture and add the eggs.

Knead lightly. Roll out into a 30 × 40 cm (12 × 16 inch) sheet.

Combine the butter, sugar and cardamom or vanilla. Spread over the dough and roll up. Cut into slices. Place, cut side up, in muffin tins or paper baking cups. Let rise for around an hour at room temperature.

Brush with beaten egg. Sprinkle with almonds. Bake on the center oven rack for 8 minutes.

RIMBO ROLLS *25 balls*

■ *Oven temp: 250°C (450°F), convection 225°C (425°F)*

25 g (1 ounce) fresh yeast or 1 tablespoon active dry yeast
2 dl (1 cup) cold milk
200 g (1 cup) stick margarine or butter, softened
1 tablespoon sugar
approx. 6 dl (2½ cups) all-purpose flour
Filling:
75 g (5 tablespoons) stick margarine or butter
2 tablespoons sugar
1½ teaspoons vanilla sugar or 1 teaspoon vanilla extract
Brushing and garnish:
beaten egg, pearl sugar, chopped almonds

▶ Crumble the yeast in a bowl. Add a little milk, stirring until dissolved. Add the remaining ingredients, kneading until smooth. Roll into a 40 cm (16 inch) square. Beat butter, sugar and vanilla until fluffy. Cut the dough into 25 squares and top each with a spoonful of butter mixture. Pinch together and place in baking cups. Let rise for around 2 hours at room temperature.

Brush with egg and sprinkle with sugar and almonds, if desired. Bake on the center oven rack for 5–8 minutes.

Rimbo Rolls

Maja's Danish Braids

MAJA'S DANISH BRAIDS *3 braids*

☆ This recipe won a prize in 1984.

■ *Oven temp: 250°C (450°F), convection 225°C (425°F)*

2 eggs
½ teaspoon salt
2 tablespoons sugar
50 g (1¾ ounces) fresh yeast or 2 tablespoons active dry yeast
5 dl (2 cups) all-purpose flour
200 g (scant 1 cup) cold stick margarine or butter
Filling:
100 g (7 tablespoons) stick margarine or butter, softened
1 dl (½ cup) sugar
50 g (3 tablespoons) diced citron
1 dl (½ cup) raisins
1 tablespoon ground cardamom
Brushing and glaze:
1 egg, lightly beaten
¾ dl (⅓ cup) powdered sugar
½ tablespoon water

▶ Whisk the eggs lightly and add the salt and sugar. Crumble the yeast into the egg mixture. Cut the flour and butter together until granular. Add the egg mixture and knead lightly together. Divide into three pieces of equal size.

Roll each into a rope and flatten with a rolling pin. The rope should be as long as the baking sheet and around 10 cm (4 inches) wide. Place on a greased or parchment-lined baking sheet.

Combine the ingredients for the filling and spoon ⅓ along the center of each piece of dough. Fold both sides toward the middle, but leave the center strip of filling exposed. Cover and let rise in a cool place for around an hour.

Brush with beaten egg. Bake on the center oven rack for around 8 minutes.

Stir the powdered sugar and water together and drizzle over the pastries. Cut into strips and serve while slightly warm or completely cooled.

Margareta Cake, page 71

Butter Cakes ▶

For the best cake:

Select the correct pan.
The size and shape of the pan are important for the finished cake. All recipes state the size of the pan in either volume or diameter.

Grease the pan well.
Use soft butter or stick margarine, which forms a thicker layer than melted fat.

Does the pan have to be floured? It is not necessary to flour the pans, but that does improve the surface of the cake. Fine breadcrumbs are best. Move the pan around so that the entire surface is covered. Shake out the rest. Farina, ground nuts, coconut or flour also can be used instead of crumbs.

Beat until light yellow and very thick. Beat the eggs and sugar until light and porous, but do not beat for more than 3–4 minutes with an electric mixer, which beats 3–5 times harder than a person can beat by hand. If the batter is overbeaten, the finished cake may sink.

Beat the butter and sugar until light and fluffy. The butter should be softened. The butter and sugar should be beaten together until loose and porous. Add the eggs, one at a time, and beat well after each egg.

Carefully blend in the flour. Carefully fold the flour into the egg mixture. Do not overmix, as the air that has been mixed into the batter can deflate and the cake will be compact.

7

8

9 **Let the cake rest.**
Never remove a newly baked cake from its pan. Let it rest for at least 5 minutes on a rack before removing from the pan, or it can stick.

Do not overfill the pan. Spread the batter over the entire pan, using a spatula or turning the pan so that the filling spreads evenly. The pan should not be more than ⅔ full. The cake batter needs room to expand.

Do not open the oven door until the latter part of the baking time. And don't slam the door! The cake is finished baking when it begins to shrink from the sides of the pan. Test with a skewer or wooden pick. Insert it into the middle of the cake. If it comes out clean, the cake is done.

Carefully remove the cake from the pan. Loosen around the edges with a knife. Turn out onto a rack. If the cake sticks to the pan, dip a towel in cold water and place it over the pan. Let cool the cake covered or in the pan to retain moisture.

10

BERRY MUFFINS *12 muffins*

■ *Oven temp: 200°C (400°F), convection 175°C (350°F)*
100 g (7 tablespoons) stick margarine or butter, softened
1½ dl (⅔ cup) sugar
4 eggs
1 teaspoon vanilla sugar or ½ teaspoon vanilla extract
5 dl (2 cups) all-purpose flour
1 teaspoon baking powder
1 dl (⅓ cup) milk
Filling: 1½ dl (⅔ cup) fresh berries, such as blueberries or raspberries

▶ Beat the butter and sugar until light and fluffy. Add the eggs, one at a time, beating well after each. Stir in the vanilla.

Combine flour and baking powder and add with the milk. Spoon into muffin tins or paper baking cups.

Place a few berries in the center of each muffin.

Bake on the center oven shelf for 15–20 minutes. Let cool.

APPLE MUFFINS *12 muffins*

Substitute 1–2 thinly sliced apples for the berries. Press them into the batter and sprinkle with a mixture of ½ teaspoon cinnamon and 1 tablespoon sugar. Bake on the center oven shelf for 15 minutes.

GLAZED CARROT MUFFINS *12 muffins*

■ *Oven temp: 200°C (400°F), convection 175°C (350°F)*
2 eggs
2 dl (¾ cup) sugar
1½ dl (scant ⅔ cup) safflower oil
50 g (½ cup) chopped walnuts
2 medium carrots, grated
1 teaspoon cinnamon
1¾ dl (¾ cup) all-purpose flour
1 teaspoon baking powder
Frosting:
50 g (3 tablespoons) stick margarine or butter, softened
75 g (5 tablespoons) cream cheese, room temperature
1 dl (½ cup) powdered sugar
½ teaspoon vanilla

▶ Grease muffin tins well.

Beat the eggs and sugar until light yellow and very thick, preferably with an electric mixer. Beat in the oil and fold in the nuts and carrots. Combine the dry ingredients and fold into the egg mixture. Spoon into the tin. Do not fill more than ¾ full.

Bake on the center oven shelf for around 20 minutes. Let cool completely.

For the frosting, beat all the ingredients until light and fluffy. Spread over the muffins. Pictured on page 63.

Apple Muffins

ALMOND MUFFINS *12 muffins*

■ *Oven temp: 200°C (400°F), convection 175°C (325°F)*

Thinly sliced almonds, lightly crushed
200 g (7 ounces) almond paste
2 eggs
1 dl (½ cup) all-purpose flour
1 teaspoon baking powder

Garnish:
grated semi-sweet chocolate

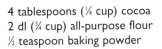

▶ Grease metal muffin tins well. Sprinkle with lightly crushed sliced almonds.

Grate the almond paste and beat with the eggs until smooth. Add the dry ingredients, mixing until combined. Pour into the prepared tins.

Bake on the center oven shelf for around 10 minutes.

Sprinkle a little grated chocolate over the warm muffins and spread to glaze. Sprinkle with crushed almonds. Let cool completely.

CHOCOLATE MUFFINS *12 muffins*

■ *Oven temp: 200°C (400°F), convection 175°C (350°F)*

100 g (6 tablespoons) stick margarine or butter
2 eggs
2½ dl (1 cup) sugar
1½ teaspoons vanilla sugar or 1 teaspoon vanilla extract
pinch salt
4 tablespoons (¼ cup) cocoa
2 dl (¾ cup) all-purpose flour
½ teaspoon baking powder

▶ Grease muffin tins or place paper baking cups in the tins.

Melt the butter and let it cool. Beat the eggs and sugar until light yellow and very thick. Add the remaining ingredients, adding the butter last. Pour into the tin. Do not fill more than ¾ full. Bake on the center oven shelf for around 10 minutes.

SPICE MUFFINS *15–20 muffins*

■ *Oven temp: 200°C (400°F), convection 175°C (350°F)*

100 g (7 tablespoons) stick margarine or butter
2 eggs
3 dl (1¼ cups) sugar
1 teaspoon ground cardamom
2 teaspoons cinnamon
½ teaspoon ginger
1 dl (⅓ cup) raisins, if desired
3 dl (1¼ cups) all-purpose flour
1 teaspoon baking powder
1 dl (⅓ cup) cream or milk

▶ Grease muffin tins or place paper baking cups in the tins.

Melt the butter and let it cool. Beat the eggs and sugar until light yellow and very thick. Add the spices and raisins. Combine the flour and baking powder and add alternately with the milk and melted butter. Pour into the prepared tin. Bake on the center oven shelf for around 15 minutes.

SPONGE CAKE

- *Oven temp: 175 °C (350 °F), convection 175 °C (350 °F)*

50–75 g (3–5 tablespoons) stick margarine
  or butter
2 eggs
2 dl (¾ cup) sugar
2 teaspoons vanilla sugar or 1 teaspoon
  vanilla extract or grated zest of ½ lemon
3 dl (1¼ cups) all-purpose flour
2 teaspoons baking powder
1 dl (⅓ cup) milk or water

▶ Grease and flour a loaf pan or a 1½ liter (6 cup) ring pan.

Melt the butter and let it cool. Or soften the butter to room temperature.

Beat the eggs and sugar until light yellow and very thick. Stir in the vanilla or lemon zest. Combine the flour and baking powder and add alternately with the butter and milk, stirring until thoroughly combined. Pour into the prepared pan.

Bake on a low oven rack for 40–50 minutes.

LACY CAKE

- *Oven temp: 175 °C (350 °F), convection 175 °C (350 °F)*

1 batch Sponge Cake batter
Glaze:
2 tablespoons stick margarine or butter
1 dl (⅓ cup) sugar
2 tablespoons cream

▶ Grease and flour a 24 cm (10 inch) spring-form pan.

Prepare the recipe for Sponge Cake but use 75 g (5 tablespoons) butter. Pour the batter into the prepared pan. Bake for 30–35 minutes.

Combine all the ingredients for the glaze. Spread over the cake. Return to the oven until golden.

EGGLESS SPONGE CAKE

An easy-to-bake sponge with a dense crumb.

- ■ *Oven temp: 200°C (400°F), convection 175°C (350°F)*

4 ½ dl (1 ¾ cups) all-purpose flour
3 dl (1 ¼ cups) sugar
2 tablespoons cornstarch
1 tablespoon baking powder
50 g (¼ cup) stick margarine or butter
2 ½ dl (1 cup) milk
1 tablespoon orange juice
2 teaspoons vanilla sugar or 1 teaspoon
   vanilla extract

▶ Grease and flour a 1 ½ liter (6 cup) loaf pan or a 22 cm (9 inch) round or ring pan. Combine the dry ingredients. Melt the butter and add with the remaining ingredients, mixing well. The batter will be very lumpy. Pour into the prepared pan.

Bake on a low oven rack for around 45 minutes. Let cool for at least 5 minutes before removing from the pan.

LIGHT SPONGE CAKE

Also called Moss Cake because of its texture. Good as a torte base.

- ■ *Oven temp: 200°C (400°F), convection 175°C (350°F)*

2 eggs
2 dl (¾ cup) sugar
2 teaspoons vanilla sugar or 1 teaspoon
   vanilla extract or grated zest of ½ lemon
1 ½ dl (⅔ cup) all-purpose flour
1 dl (½ cup) potato starch or cornstarch
2 teaspoons baking powder
1 dl (⅓ cup) hot water

▶ Grease and flour a 1 ½ liter (6 cup) loaf pan or a 20 cm (8 inch) round or ring pan.

Beat the eggs and sugar until light yellow and very thick. Stir in the vanilla or lemon zest. Combine the dry ingredients and fold into the egg mixture. Stir in the water, mixing lightly until combined. Pour into the prepared pan.

Bake on a low oven rack for 25–30 minutes.

KERSTIN'S CAKE

☆ This recipe won a prize in 1945 and is also called Sunshine Cake.

■ *Oven temp: 175°C (350°F), convection 175°C (350°F)*

125 g (½ cup) stick margarine or butter
3 eggs
3 dl (1 ¼ cups) sugar
3 dl (1 ¼ cups) all-purpose flour
1 teaspoon baking powder

Garnish:
20 blanched almonds

▶ Grease and flour a 24 cm (10 inch) spring-form pan.

Melt the butter and let it cool.

Beat the eggs and sugar until light yellow and very thick. Combine the flour and baking powder and add alternately with the butter. Pour into the pan.

Bake on a low oven rack for around 10 minutes.

Halve the almonds lengthwise and arrange over the batter. Continue baking for 20–30 minutes more.

Let cool for at least 5 minutes before removing from the pan.

OLD-FASHIONED POUND CAKE

■ *Oven temp: 150°C (300°F), convection 150°C (300°F)*

1 ½ dl (⅔ cup) all-purpose flour
1 dl (½ cup) potato starch or cornstarch
1 teaspoon baking powder
150 g (scant ⅔ cup) stick margarine or butter, softened
3 eggs
1 ½ dl (⅔ cup) sugar
1 tablespoon cognac or grated zest and juice of 1 lemon

▶ Grease and flour a 1 liter (4 cup) loaf pan or small ring pan.

Combine the dry ingredients. Add the butter, beating until smooth.

Beat the eggs and sugar until light yellow and very thick. Whisk into the butter mixture with the cognac, mixing well.

Pour into the prepared pan, pushing the batter up the sides slightly with a spatula.

Bake on a low oven rack for around 50 minutes

Let cool for at least 5 minutes before removing from the pan. Cover and Let cool completely.

Cut into thin slices. This cake tastes even better if allowed to mature for a few days.

Kerstin's Cake

Old-Fashioned Pound Cake

TYRA'S GINGER CAKE

■ *Oven temp: 175°C (350°F), convection 175°C (350°F)*

150 g (scant ⅔ cup) stick margarine or butter, softened
2 dl (¾ cup) sugar
3 eggs
1 medium apple
grated zest and juice of 1 lemon
2–3 tablespoons chopped candied ginger
3 dl (1 ¼ cups) all-purpose flour
2 teaspoons baking powder

▶ Grease and flour a 1 ½ liter (6 cup) loaf pan or ring pan.

Beat the butter and sugar until light and fluffy, preferably with an electric mixer. Add the eggs, one at a time, beating well after each.

Grate the apple, with peel if desired, and add along with the lemon zest and juice.

Combine the remaining ingredients and fold into the egg mixture. Pour into the prepared pan.

Bake on a low oven rack for around 45 minutes.

Let cool for at least 5 minutes before removing from the pan. Let cool completely on a rack.

SAFFRON CAKE

☆ This recipe won a prize in 1984.

■ *Oven temp: 175°C (350°F), convection 175°C (350°F)*

200 g (¾ cup) stick margarine or butter
½ gram (large pinch) saffron
1 sugar cube
2 eggs
3 dl (1 ¼ cups) sugar
1 ½ dl (⅔ cup) milk
4 dl (1 ⅔ cups) all-purpose flour
2 teaspoons baking powder
powdered sugar, if desired

▶ Grease and flour a 24 cm (10 inch) springform pan.

Melt the butter and let it cool. Crush the saffron with the sugar cube in a mortar.

Beat the eggs and sugar until light yellow and very thick. Add the saffron, butter and milk. Combine the dry ingredients and add, beating well. Pour into the prepared pan.

Bake on a low oven rack for around 45 minutes.

Just before serving, sift powdered sugar over the cake.

Tyra's Ginger Cake

GERMAN LEMON CAKE

- *Oven temp: 175°C (350°F), convection 175°C (350°F)*

150 g (scant ⅔ cup) stick margarine or butter
3 eggs
2 dl (¾ cup) sugar
pinch salt
grated zest of ½ lemon
3 dl (1 ¼ cups) all-purpose flour
1 teaspoon baking powder

Glaze:
2 dl (¾ cup) powdered sugar
juice of 1 lemon
2 tablespoons water

▶ Grease and flour a 1 ½ liter (6 cup) ring pan.

Melt the butter and let it cool.

Beat the eggs, sugar, salt and lemon zest until light yellow and very thick. Stir in the butter and fold in the dry ingredients. Pour into the prepared pan.

Bake on a low oven rack for around 45 minutes.

Let cool for around 5 minutes before removing from the pan onto a serving platter.

Combine the ingredients for the glaze. Stick holes in the cake with a skewer. Pour the glaze in the holes. Serve the cake chilled.

ORANGE-CHOCOLATE CAKE

- *Oven temp: 175°C (350°F), convection 175°C (350°F)*

150 g (scant ⅔ cup) stick margarine or butter, softened
2½ dl (1 cup) sugar
3 eggs
4 dl (1 ⅔ cups) all-purpose flour
1 teaspoon baking powder
1 teaspoon vanilla sugar or ½ teaspoon vanilla extract
1 dl (⅓ cup) orange juice concentrate
100 g (½ cup) semi-sweet chocolate chips

▶ Grease and flour a 1 ½ liter (6 cup) loaf or ring pan.

Beat the butter and sugar until light and fluffy. Add the eggs, one at a time, beating well after each. Combine the dry ingredients and add alternately with the orange juice concentrate. Fold in the chocolate chips. Pour into the prepared pan.

Bake on a low oven rack for 50–60 minutes.

Let cool for 5 minutes before removing from the pan.

Drizzle melted chocolate over the cake for a festive touch.

BANANA CAKE

- *Oven temp: 175°C (350°F),*
  convection 175°C (350°F)

100 g (7 tablespoons) stick margarine or butter, softened
3 dl (1 ¼ cups) sugar
2 eggs
5 dl (2 cups) all-purpose flour
1 teaspoon baking powder
1 teaspoon baking soda
1 teaspoon ginger
2 teaspoons cinnamon
2 large bananas
½ dl (3 tablespoons) cold coffee

▶ Grease and flour a 1 ½ liter (6 cup) loaf or
ring pan.

Beat the butter and sugar until light and
fluffy. Add the eggs, one at a time, beating
well after each. Combine the dry ingredients
and spices and add.

Mash the bananas and add with the coffee.
Pour into the prepared pan.

Bake on a low oven rack for one hour.

Let cool for 5 minutes before removing
from the pan.

FYRI'S CAKE

Also called Apple Sponge Cake. Serve with
whipped cream or ice cream

- *Oven temp: 175°C (350°F), convection 175°C
  (350°F)*

125 g (½ cup) stick margarine or butter
1 ½ dl (⅔ cup) sugar
2 eggs
2 ½ dl (1 cup) all-purpose flour
½ teaspoon baking powder
2 tablespoons milk
3–4 medium apples
1–2 tablespoons sugar
1 teaspoon cinnamon, if desired

▶ Grease and flour a 24 cm (10 inch) spring-
form pan.

Melt the butter and let it cool.

Beat the sugar into the butter. Add the
eggs, one at a time, beating well after each.
Combine the dry ingredients and add alternately with the milk. Pour into the prepared
pan.

Peel the apples, if desired, and cut into thin
wedges. Push the wedges into the batter in a
pinwheel pattern. Sprinkle with sugar mixed
with cinnamon, if desired.

Bake on a low oven rack for around 30–40
minutes.

FRUIT CAKE

This moist cake should be stored for a few days before serving in thin slices.

- Oven temp: 150°C (300°F), convection 150°C (300°F)

50 g (3 tablespoons) chopped candied citron or pineapple
50 g (3 tablespoons) chopped candied orange peel
10–15 candied cherries
3½ dl (1½ cups) all-purpose flour
200 g (¾ cup) stick margarine or butter, softened
2½ dl (1 cup) sugar
3 eggs
½ teaspoon baking powder
1 dl (½ cup) raisins

▶ Grease and flour a 1½ liter (6 cup) tube pan. Combine the fruit with a little of the flour to keep it from sticking together and sinking in the cake.

Beat the butter and sugar until light and fluffy. Add the eggs, one at a time, beating well after each. Combine the remaining flour with the baking powder and add. Fold in the fruit. Pour into the prepared pan.

Bake on a low oven rack for around one hour.

CURRANT CAKE

This cake should be stored for a couple of days before serving.

- Oven temp: 150°C (300°F), convection 150°C (300°F)

400 g (2¾ cups) currants
200 g (¾ cup) stick margarine or butter, softened
2 dl (¾ cup) sugar
4 eggs
2 teaspoons cinnamon
grated zest of
  1 lemon
¼ teaspoon almond extract
3½ dl (1½ cups) all-purpose flour
1 teaspoon baking powder
2 tablespoons lemon juice and 1 tablespoon water or 3 tablespoons cognac

▶ Grease and flour a 2 liter (8 cup) loaf or tube pan.

Rinse the currants in hot water, if desired. Dry well. Toss them with a little of the flour.

Beat the butter and sugar until light and fluffy. Add the eggs, one at a time, beating well after each.

Add the dry ingredients, then the liquid, mixing well. Fold in the currants last. Pour into the prepared pan.

Bake on a low oven rack for around one hour.

Variation: Substitute raisins for the currants.

Pictured at right: Carrot Almond Cake, page 71 top; Gooseberry Cake, page 64, left; and Frosted Carrot Muffins, page 54.

ENGLISH FRUIT CAKE

- *Oven temp: 150°C (300°F), convection 150°C (300°F)*
- 150 g (5 ounces) dried figs (around 1 cup diced)
- 3 tablespoons cognac
- 200 g (¾ cup) stick margarine or butter, softened
- 3 dl (1¼ cups) dark brown sugar
- 4 eggs
- 1 dl (½ cup) raisins
- 15 candied red cherries, halved
- ½ teaspoon ground cloves
- ¼ teaspoon ground nutmeg
- 1 tablespoon cinnamon
- 1 teaspoon ginger
- grated zest of 1 lemon
- 3½ dl (1½ cups) all-purpose flour
- ½ teaspoon baking powder

▶ Grease and flour a 1½ liter (6 cup) ring pan.

Dice the figs and soak in cognac for at least 2 hours.

Beat the butter and sugar until light and fluffy. Add the eggs, one at a time, beating well after each.

Stir in the fruit, then the flour mixed with the baking powder, mixing well. Pour into the prepared pan.

Bake on a rack on the bottom of the oven for 1¼–1½ hours.

GOOSEBERRY CAKE

- *Oven temp: 175°C (350°F), convection 175°C (350°F)*
- 4 eggs
- 75 g (5 tablespoons) stick margarine or butter, softened
- 2 dl (¾ cup) sugar
- 3 dl (1¼ cups) all-purpose flour
- 2 teaspoons baking powder
- 3–4 dl (1½ cups) fresh or frozen gooseberries
- 2 tablespoons sugar
- *Garnish:* powdered sugar

▶ Grease and flour a 22 cm (9 inch) springform pan.

Separate the eggs, reserving the whites in a large mixing bowl. Beat the egg yolks, butter and sugar until light and fluffy. Combine the flour and baking powder and add.

Beat the egg whites until stiff. Mix half into the batter, then carefully fold in the rest. Pour half the batter into the pan. Arrange an even layer of berries over the batter. Top with the remaining batter. Sprinkle with sugar.

Bake on a lower oven rack for around 1 hour. Let cool for 5 minutes on a rack before removing from the pan.

Let cool completely. Sift over a little powdered sugar just before serving.

Pictured on page 63.

HONEY, FRUIT AND NUT CAKE

☆ This recipe won a prize in 1965.

■ *Oven temp: 175°C (350°F),*
  convection 175°C (350°F)

200 g (¾ cup) stick margarine or butter, softened
1 dl (½ cup) sugar
1 dl (⅓ cup) honey
200 g (1 scant cup) creamed cottage cheese
2 large eggs
150 g (5 ounces/around 8) dried figs (around 1 cup diced)
100 g (3 ounces/around 15) pitted prunes (around ⅔ cup diced)
125 g (1 cup) ground walnuts or hazelnuts
4 tablespoons (¼ cup) orange marmalade
4 dl (1 ⅔ cups) all-purpose flour
2 teaspoons baking powder

Garnish:
2 dl (¾ cup) powdered sugar
lemon juice

▶ Grease and flour a 1 ½ liter (6 cup) ring pan.

Beat the butter, sugar and honey until light and fluffy. Sieve the cottage cheese and add, beating well. Separate the eggs, reserving the whites in a large mixing bowl. Add the egg yolks, one at a time, beating well after each. Dice the figs and prunes and add, along with the nuts and marmalade. Combine the flour and baking powder and add, mixing until well combined.

Beat the egg whites until stiff and carefully fold into the batter. Pour into the prepared pan.

Bake on a low oven rack for around 1 hour.

Let cool completely. Drizzle with glaze made from powdered sugar mixed with a few drops of lemon juice.

GRANDMOTHER'S CHOCOLATE CAKE

■ *Oven temp: 175 °C (350 °F), convection 175 °C (350 °F)*

1 dl (½ cup) cocoa
2 dl (1 cup) milk
1 dl (½ cup) sugar
125 g (½ cup) stick margarine or butter, softened
1 ½ dl (¾ cup) sugar
2 eggs
1 ½ tablespoons vanilla sugar or 2 teaspoons vanilla extract
3 ½ dl (1 ¾ cups) all-purpose flour

▶ Grease and flour a 1 ¼ liter (5 cup/8 inch round) pan. Combine the cocoa, milk and first amount of sugar in a saucepan and heat to boiling. Remove from the heat and let cool.

Beat the butter and sugar until light and fluffy. Beat in the eggs and vanilla. Combine the flour and baking powder and add alternately with the cocoa mixture. Pour into the prepared pan.

Bake on a low oven rack for around 1 hour.

Grandmother's Chocolate Cake

CHOCOLATE WALNUT CAKE

■ *Oven temp: 175 °C (350 °F), convection 175 °C (350 °F)*

100 g (4 ounces) semi-sweet chocolate
3 eggs
150 g (¾ cup) stick margarine or butter, softened
2 dl (1 cup) sugar
2 teaspoons vanilla sugar or 1 teaspoon vanilla extract
4 dl (2 cups) all-purpose flour
2 teaspoons baking powder
2 dl (1 cup) light cream or milk
1 ½ dl (¾ cup) coarsely chopped walnuts

▶ Grease and flour a 1 ¼ liter (8 cup) loaf or tube pan.

Melt the chocolate (see page 122) over a water bath or in the microwave oven and let cool.

Beat the butter and sugar until light and fluffy. Separate the eggs, reserving the whites in a large mixer bowl. Add the yolks, one at a time, beating well after each. Add the vanilla. Beat the egg whites until stiff. Combine the flour and baking powder and add alternately with the melted chocolate and cream. Stir in the nuts, then fold in the egg whites. Pour into the prepared pan.

Bake on a low oven rack for around 1 hour.

Variation: Substitute hazelnuts or blanched almonds for the walnuts.

Chocolate Walnut Cake

TIGER CAKE

Also called Marble Cake.

- *Oven temp: 175 °C (350 °F), convection 175 °C (350 °F)*

200 g (¾ cup) stick margarine or butter, softened
2 ½ dl (1 cup) sugar
3 eggs
4 dl (1 ⅔ cups) all-purpose flour
1 teaspoon baking powder
1 dl (½ cup) light cream or milk

Addition:
2 tablespoons cocoa
1 tablespoon vanilla sugar or 1 ½ teaspoons vanilla extract
or grated zest of ½–1 lemon or orange

▶ Grease and flour a 1 ½ liter (6 cup) loaf pan.

Beat the butter and sugar until light and fluffy. Add the eggs, one at a time, beating well after each. Combine the flour and baking powder and add alternately with the cream.

Remove around ⅓ of the batter and mix with the cocoa. Add vanilla or peel to the remaining batter.

Pour half the light batter into the prepared pan, then the dark batter. Top with the remaining light batter. Draw a fork through the batter for a marbled texture.

Bake on a low oven rack for around 1 hour.

SAFFRON MARBLE CAKE

This recipe won a prize in 1985.

- *Oven temp: 175 °C (350 °F), convection 175 °C (350 °F)*

125 g (½ cup) stick margarine or butter
5 dl (2 cups) all-purpose flour
1 teaspoon baking powder
1 teaspoon baking soda
2 eggs
2 ½ dl (1 cup) sugar
2 ½ dl (1 cup) sour cream
½ dl (¼ cup) raisins
1 tablespoon cocoa
¼ gram (pinch) saffron stirred into 1 teaspoon water

▶ Grease and flour a 1 ½ liter (6 cup) loaf pan.

Melt the butter and let it cool. Combine the dry ingredients.

Beat the eggs and sugar until light yellow and very thick. Add the buttermilk and melted butter alternately with the dry ingredients. Fold in the raisins.

Divide the batter in half. Stir the cocoa into one half, the saffron into the other. Layer the batters in the prepared pan. Draw a fork through the batter for a marbled texture.

Bake on a low oven rack for around 1 hour.

CINNAMON CAKE

☆ This recipe won a prize in 1965.

■ *Oven temp: 175°C (350°F),*
convection 175°C (350°F)

3 eggs
2 dl (¾ cup) sugar
2½ dl (1 cup) all-purpose flour
2 teaspoons baking powder
1 tablespoon cinnamon
75 g (5 tablespoons) stick margarine or butter
1 dl (⅓ cup) water
Garnish:
½ dl (¼ cup) sliced almonds

▶ Grease and flour a 1½ liter (8 inch) round pan.

Beat the eggs and sugar until light yellow and very thick. Combine the dry ingredients and add.

Heat the butter and water to boiling and add, mixing well. Pour into the prepared pan.

Sprinkle with the almonds.

Bake on a low oven rack for around 45 minutes.

Let cool for 5 minutes, then remove from the pan.

Tip: This cake can be baked in a loaf pan, but increase the flour to 3 dl (1¼ cups).

PRIORY GINGERBREAD

☆ This recipe won a prize in 1945.

■ *Oven temp: 175°C (350°F),*
convection 175°C (350°F)

100 g (7 tablespoons) stick margarine or butter
2 eggs
2 dl (¾ cup) sugar
1½ dl (⅔ cup) sour cream
1½ teaspoons ginger
1½ teaspoons ground cloves
2 teaspoons cinnamon
3 dl (1¼ cups) all-purpose flour
1 teaspoon baking soda or 2 teaspoons baking powder

▶ Grease and flour a 1½ liter (6 cup) loaf pan. Melt the butter and let it cool.

Beat the eggs and sugar until light yellow and very thick. Add the remaining ingredients, mixing well. Pour into the prepared pan.

Bake on a low oven rack for around 45 minutes.

LINGONBERRY SPICE CAKE

■ *Oven temp: 175 °C (350 °F),*
  convection 175 °C (350 °F)

100 g (7 tablespoons) stick margarine or butter
2 eggs
3 dl (1 ¼ cups) dark brown sugar
2 teaspoons cinnamon
1 ½ teaspoons ground cardamom
1 teaspoon ginger
3 ½ dl (1 ½ cups) all-purpose flour
1 teaspoon baking soda or 2 teaspoons baking powder
1 dl (½ cup) cultured buttermilk
1 dl (⅓ cup) lingonberry preserves

▶ Grease and flour a 1 ½ liter (6 cup) loaf pan. Melt the butter and let it cool.

Beat the eggs and sugar until light yellow and very thick. Combine the dry ingredients and add alternately with the buttermilk, butter and preserves. Pour into the prepared pan.

Bake on a low oven rack for around 1 hour.

MARGIT'S SPICE CAKE

■ *Oven temp: 175 °C (350 °F),*
  convection 175 °C (350 °F)

1 ½ dl (⅔ cup) water
125 g (½ cup) stick margarine or butter
2 tablespoons instant coffee granules
2 eggs
1 ½ dl (⅔ cup) sugar
1 ½ dl (⅔ cup) light or dark corn/sugar syrup
1 tablespoon cinnamon
½ teaspoon ground cloves
1 teaspoon baking soda
4 ½ dl (2 cups) all-purpose flour
1 dl (½ cup) currants or 1 ½ dl (⅔ cup) raisins

▶ Grease and flour a 2 liter (8 cup) tube pan. Heat the water, butter and coffee granules to boiling. Let cool.

Separate the eggs, reserving the whites in a medium mixer bowl. Beat the egg yolks, sugar and syrup until light and frothy. Beat the whites until stiff. Combine the dry ingredients and add alternately with the coffee mixture. Fold in the currants or raisins, then fold in the egg whites. Pour into the prepared pan.

Bake on a low oven rack for around 1 hour.

MINNIE'S ALMOND CAKE

☆ This recipe won a prize in 1945.

- *Oven temp: 175 °C (350 °F), convection 175 °C (350 °F)*

125 g (½ cup) stick margarine or butter
4 eggs
2 ¾ dl (1 cup) sugar
1 dl (⅓ cup) light cream or milk
100 g (1 cup) ground almonds
1 ½ dl (⅔ cup) dry breadcrumbs
grated zest of 1 orange
powdered sugar

▶ Grease and flour a 22 cm (9 inch) spring-form pan.

Melt the butter and let it cool.

Separate the eggs, reserving the whites in a large mixer bowl.

Beat the egg yolks and sugar until light yellow and very thick.

Stir in the melted butter and cream.

Combine ground almonds, breadcrumbs and orange zest and stir into the batter.

Beat the egg whites until stiff and carefully fold into the batter. Pour into the prepared pan.

Bake on a low oven rack for around 1 hour.

Just before serving, sprinkle with powdered sugar.

NUT RIBBON CAKE

- *Oven temp: 175 °C (350 °F), convection 175 °C (350 °F)*

100 g (7 tablespoons) stick margarine or butter, softened
2 dl (¾ cup) sugar
2 eggs
¼ teaspoon almond extract
5 dl (2 cups) all-purpose flour
2 teaspoons baking powder
¼ teaspoon salt
2 ½ dl (1 cup) sour cream

Filling:
50 g (3 tablespoons) stick margarine or butter
1 ½ dl (⅔ cup) dark brown sugar
2 teaspoons cinnamon
2 tablespoon all-purpose flour
100 g (¾ cup) chopped hazelnuts or walnuts

▶ Grease and flour a 2 liter (8 cup) loaf pan.

Beat the butter and sugar until light and fluffy. Add the eggs, one at a time, beating well after each. Add the almond extract.

Combine the flour, baking powder and salt. Add alternately with the sour cream, beating well.

Melt the butter for the filling and mix with the remaining ingredients.

Spread half the cake batter in the prepared pan. Spoon the filling evenly over the batter and top with the remaining batter.

Bake on a low oven rack for 45–50 minutes.

Let cool for 5 minutes before removing from the pan.

MARGARETA CAKE

■ *Oven temp: 175°C (350°F),*
   convection 175°C (350°F)

100 g (4 ounces) almond paste
200 g (1 cup) stick margarine or butter
1 dl (½ cup) sugar
1 teaspoon grated orange zest
4 eggs
1 ½ dl (¾ cup) all-purpose flour
½ dl (¼ cup) potato starch or cornstarch
1 teaspoon baking powder

Glaze:
Around 1 dl (⅓ cup) orange marmalade
1 dl (⅓ cup) powdered sugar
1 ½ tablespoons orange juice
1 dl (⅓ cup) sliced almonds

▶ Grease and flour a 1 ½ liter (6 cup) decorative pan.

Grate the almond paste by hand or in a food processor. Add the butter, sugar and zest and beat until smooth.

Add the eggs, one at a time, beating well after each. Combine the dry ingredients and fold into the egg mixture.

Pour into the prepared pan.

Bake on the lowest oven rack for around 50 minutes. Let cool for 10 minutes before removing from the pan.

Spread the marmalade over the top and sides of the cake. Let cool completely.

Combine the powdered sugar and orange juice to make a thin glaze. Toast the almonds in the oven after the cake is removed. Spread the glaze over the cake and sprinkle with almonds around the sides.

Pictured on page 51.

CARROT-ALMOND CAKE

This cake is easy to make with a food processor.

■ *Oven temp: 175°C (350°F),*
   convection 175°C (350°F)

3 carrots (around 200 g/8 ounces)
50 g (½ cup) almonds
2 eggs
2 dl (1 cup) sugar
1 teaspoon vanilla sugar or ½ teaspoon vanilla extract
½ teaspoon cinnamon
½ teaspoon ginger
1 teaspoon baking powder
½ teaspoon baking soda
2 dl (1 cup) all-purpose flour
1 dl (½ cup) corn oil
powdered sugar

▶ Grease and flour a 1 ½ liter (6 cup) loaf pan.

Peel the carrots and cut into small chunks. Place in a food processor with the almonds and process for 30 seconds, until all is finely chopped. Add the eggs, sugar and vanilla and process for 30 seconds.

Combine the dry ingredients. Using the pulse button, add the oil and the dry ingredients, processing until just combined. Pour into the prepared pan.

Bake on a low oven rack for around 45 minutes.

Let cool for 10 minutes before removing from the pan. Just before serving, sift powdered sugar over the cake, or top with a glaze.

Pictured on page 63.

NUT CAKE

- *Oven temp: 175°C (350°F), convection 175°C (350°F)*

125 g (½ cup) stick margarine or butter, softened
1 ½ dl (⅔ cup) sugar
2 eggs
75 g (¾ cup) ground nuts
1 ½ dl (⅔ cup) all-purpose flour
½ teaspoon baking powder

▶ Grease and flour a 1 liter (4 cup) loaf pan or 8 inch round cake pan.

Beat the butter and sugar until light and fluffy. Add the eggs, one at a time, beating well after each. Combine the nuts, flour and baking powder and carefully fold into the egg mixture. Pour into the prepared pan.

Bake on a low oven rack for around 30 minutes.

COCONUT CAKE

- *Oven temp: 175°C (350°F), convection 175°C (350°F)*

150 g (¾ cup) stick margarine or butter
3 eggs
2 dl (1 cup) sugar
200 g (1 ⅔ cups) flaked coconut
50 g (3 tablespoons) finely chopped candied orange peel
50 g (¼ cup) semi-sweet chocolate mini-chips, if desired
½ dl (¼ cup) all-purpose flour
1 teaspoon baking powder

▶ Grease a 22 cm (9 inch) round cake pan and sprinkle with coconut.

Melt the butter and let it cool.

Beat the eggs and sugar until light yellow and very thick. Add the butter.

Combine the remaining ingredients and fold into the egg mixture. Pour into the prepared pan.

Bake on a low oven rack for around 30 minutes.

Dream Roll, page 76

Rolled Cakes ▶

Beat hard and bake fast

Line a baking sheet with parchment paper. Or use a shallow roasting pan or a 30 × 40 cm (12 × 16 inch) sheet cake pan. Grease the paper.

Make corners. Line a baking sheet with parchment paper. Cut into the corners of the paper and flip up to make a shallow rim.

Beat hard. Beat the eggs and sugar until really light and thick. That makes a light, porous cake. You can mix by hand, but an electric mixer does an even better job.

Remove the parchment paper easily. If the cake sticks, brush the paper with cold water to make it easier to remove.

5 **No cracks.** Roll the cake while still warm if you are filling it with preserves or berry puree. Let the cake cool before filling it with buttercream or whipped cream.

Thick or thin. Roll a long thin cake from the long side, using the paper as a guide. For bigger, more beautiful slices, roll from the short side.

JELLY ROLL

- *Oven temp: 250 °C (450 °F),
  convection 200 °C (400 °F)*

3 eggs
2 dl (1 cup) sugar
2 dl (1 cup) all-purpose flour
2 teaspoons baking powder
½ dl (¼ cup) milk or sour cream
Filling:
2 dl (1 cup) thick preserves or fruit puree

▶ Line a baking sheet or 30 × 40 cm (12 × 16 inch) sheet cake pan with parchment paper.

Beat the eggs and sugar until light yellow and very thick.

Combine the dry ingredients and fold into the egg mixture. Stir in the milk.

Spread the batter evenly over the prepared pan.

Bake on the center oven rack for around 5 minutes.

Turn the cake out onto parchment paper sprinkled with sugar. Remove the paper from the cake.

Immediately spread with filling and roll up the cake. Let cool completely, seam side down, before cutting into slices.

JELLY ROLL SLICES WITH BERRIES *10 slices*

Select berries according to the season. Frozen berries should be partially defrosted.

- *Oven temp: 250 °C (450 °F),
  convection 200 °C (400 °F)*

1 batch Jelly Roll batter
Filling:
3 dl (1 cup) whipping cream
2 dl (¾ cup) berries, such as black currants
  or blueberries
2–3 tablespoons sugar
Garnish:
whipped cream
berries, such as black or red currants or
  blueberries
sliced toasted almonds, if desired

▶ Prepare the cake base according to the recipe for Jelly Roll. Let cool completely, covered with the pan, so that it does not crack when rolled.

Whip the cream.

Mash the berries and mix in the sugar. Carefully fold the mixture into ⅔ of the cream.

Spread the filling over the cake. Roll up and cut into 10 pieces of equal size.

Garnish with a dollop of whipped cream, or pipe the cream onto the cake and garnish with whole berries. Sprinkle with almonds, if desired.

Jelly Roll

*Jelly Roll Slice
with Berries*

DREAM ROLL

- *Oven temp: 250°C (450°F), convection 200°C (400°C)*

3 eggs
1 ½ dl (⅔ cup) sugar
¾ dl (⅓ cup) potato starch or cornstarch
2 tablespoons cocoa
1 teaspoon baking powder
Filling:
100 g (7 tablespoons) stick margarine or butter
2 dl (¾ cup) powdered sugar
1 teaspoon vanilla

1 egg yolk (pasteurised) or 1 ½ tablespoons egg substitute (refrigerated or defrosted)

▶ Line a baking sheet or 30 × 40 cm (12 × 16 inch) sheet cake pan with parchment paper.

Beat the eggs and sugar until light yellow and very thick.

Combine the dry ingredients and fold into the egg mixture.

Spread the batter evenly over the prepared pan.

Bake on the center oven rack for around 5 minutes.

Turn the cake out onto parchment paper sprinkled with sugar. Remove the paper from the cake. Let cool completely.

For the filling, beat the butter and sugar until light and fluffy. Add the vanilla and beat in the egg yolk or egg substitute.

Spread the filling evenly over the cake. Roll up and place, seam side down, on a platter. Refrigerate for at least one hour before slicing.

Also pictured on page 73.

COCONUT ROLL

- *Oven temp: 250°C (450°F), convection 200°C (400°F)*

3 eggs
2 dl (¾ cup) sugar
3 dl (1 ¼ cups) flaked coconut
¾ dl (⅓ cup) potato starch or cornstarch
1 ½ teaspoons baking powder
Filling:
75 g (5 tablespoons) stick margarine or butter
1 ½ dl (⅔ cup) powdered sugar
1 ½ dl (⅔ cup) thick vanilla pudding or custard

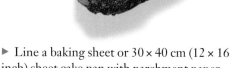

▶ Line a baking sheet or 30 × 40 cm (12 × 16 inch) sheet cake pan with parchment paper.

Beat the eggs and sugar until light yellow and very thick.

Combine the coconut, starch and baking powder and fold into the egg mixture.

Spread the batter evenly over the prepared pan.

Bake on the center oven rack for around 5 minutes.

Turn the cake out onto parchment paper sprinkled with sugar. Remove the paper from the cake. Let cool completely.

For the filling, beat the butter and sugar until fluffy. Beat in the pudding in spoonfuls.

Spread the filling evenly over the cake. Roll up and place, seam side down, on a platter. Refrigerate for at least an hour before slicing.

PUNCH ROLL

- *Oven temp. 250 °C (450 °F), convection 200 °C (400 °F)*

3 eggs
1 ½ dl (⅔ cup) sugar
2 dl (¾ cup) all-purpose flour
2 teaspoons baking powder
2 tablespoons Swedish "Punsch" (arrak-flavored spirits) or anise liqueur
1 ½ tablespoons milk

Filling:
100 g (7 tablespoons) stick margarine or butter
1 ½ dl (⅔ cup) powdered sugar
1 ½ tablespoons cocoa
½ teaspoon vanilla
1 egg yolk (pasteurised) or 1 ½ tablespoons egg substitute (refrigerated or defrosted)
½ dl (3 tablespoons) Swedish "Punsch" or anise liqueur

▶ Line a baking sheet or 30 × 40 cm (12 × 16 inch) sheet cake pan with parchment paper.

Beat the eggs and sugar until very thick. Combine the dry ingredients and fold into the egg mixture. Stir in the Punch and milk.

Spread the batter evenly over the prepared pan. Bake on the center oven shelf for around 5 minutes.

Turn the cake out onto parchment paper sprinkled with sugar. Remove the paper from the cake. Cover the cake with the baking pan and let cool completely.

Beat the butter and sugar until fluffy. Add cocoa, vanilla, egg yolk and Punch.

Spread the filling over the cake. Roll up and place, seam side down, on a platter. Refrigerate for at least an hour before slicing.

MOCHA-NUT ROLL

This wonderful cake is best when served really cold. You can even put it in the freezer for a couple of hours.

- *Oven temp: 250 °C (450 °F), convection 200 °C (400 °F)*

3 eggs
1 ½ dl (⅔ cup) sugar
100 g (1 ¼ cups) ground hazelnuts
1 tablespoon potato starch or cornstarch
2 teaspoons baking powder

Filling:
100 g (7 tablespoons) stick margarine or butter
1 ½ dl (⅔ cup) powdered sugar
1 tablespoon cocoa
1–2 teaspoons instant coffee granules
1 teaspoon vanilla
1 egg yolk (pasteurised) or 1 ½ tablespoons egg substitute (refrigerated or defrosted)

▶ Line a baking sheet or 30 × 40 cm (12 × 16 inch) sheet cake pan with parchment paper.

Beat the eggs and sugar until light yellow and very thick.

Combine the nuts, starch and baking powder and fold into the egg mixture.

Spread the batter evenly over the prepared pan.

Bake on the center oven rack for around 5 minutes.

Turn the cake out onto parchment paper sprinkled with sugar. Remove the paper from the cake. Let cool completely.

For the filling, beat the butter and sugar until fluffy. Add the cocoa and coffee. Beat in the vanilla and egg yolk.

Spread the filling evenly over the cake. Roll up and place, seam side down, on a platter. Refrigerate for at least an hour before slicing.

Serve with whipped cream.

ORANGE CREAM ROLL

■ *Oven temp: 250°C (450°F),*
   convection 200°C (400°F)
3 eggs
1 ½ dl (⅔ cup) sugar
¾ dl (⅓ cup) potato starch or cornstarch
¼ dl (2 ½ tablespoons) all-purpose flour
1 teaspoon baking powder
Orange cream:
2 gelatin sheets
1 egg
½ dl (3 tablespoons) sugar
1 ½ dl (⅔ cup) whipping cream
grated zest of ½ orange
1 ½ dl (⅔ cup) orange juice

▶ Line a baking sheet or 30 × 40 cm (12 × 16 inch) sheet cake pan with parchment paper.

Beat the eggs and sugar until light yellow and very thick.

Combine the dry ingredients and fold into the egg mixture.

Spread the batter evenly over the prepared pan.

Bake on the center oven shelf for around 5 minutes.

Turn the cake out onto parchment paper sprinkled with sugar. Remove the paper from the cake. Let cool completely.

Soak the gelatin in cold water for at least 5 minutes until softened.

Orange Cream Roll

Lingonberry Spice Roll

Combine the egg, sugar and cream in a saucepan and heat, stirring constantly, until thickened. Do not allow to boil or the egg will scramble.

Squeeze excess water from the gelatin and add to the hot cream, stirring until melted. When completely melted, add the orange zest and juice. Refrigerate for 2 hours.

Spread the cream evenly over the cake and roll up. Place, seam side down, on a platter and refrigerate for at least an hour before slicing.

LINGONBERRY SPICE ROLL

■ *Oven temp: 250°C (350°F),*
   convection 200°C (400°F)
3 eggs
1 ½ dl (⅔ cup) sugar
¾ dl (⅓ cup) potato starch or cornstarch
1 ½ tablespoons all-purpose flour
1 teaspoon baking powder
1 teaspoon cinnamon
½ teaspoon ginger
½ teaspoon ground cloves
Filling:
2 dl (¾ cup) lingonberry preserves

▶ Line a baking sheet or 30 × 40 cm (12 × 16 inch) sheet cake pan with parchment paper.

Beat the eggs and sugar until light yellow and very thick.

Combine the dry ingredients and fold into the egg mixture.

Spread the batter evenly over the prepared pan.

Bake on the center oven rack for around 5 minutes.

Turn the cake out onto parchment paper sprinkled with sugar. Remove the paper from the cake.

Immediately spread the filling over the cake and roll up. Let cool, seam side down, before slicing.

Cookies ▷

How to bake good cookies

1 Do not add all the flour at once. Save a little for rolling out.

2 Let butter cookie dough rest. Refrigerate the dough for a couple of hours for easier rolling.

Rolling out butter cookie dough. Use a cloth-covered rolling pin.

... or roll out between two layers of plastic wrap.

Baking times. Baking times in the recipes are approximate. The time can vary depending on your oven and the thickness of the cookies.

Always test-bake a couple of cookies.

Transfer the cookies to a rack for cooling. Cookies should always be completely cold before they are placed in a tin.

Tips

Stick margarine or butter?
Both work just fine. Use what you like best. Sometimes butter is better, as that "buttery" flavor adds to the cookie.

Measure the flour correctly. Use a measuring cup, dip into the flour and level it off at the rim.

Different leavening agents
1 teaspoon baking soda =
2 teaspoons baking powder
1 teaspoon hornsalt (baking ammonia) =
2 teaspoons baking powder

Brush citrus fruits well. Brush lemons and oranges in warm water before grating the zest.

Store in plastic wrap. Rolls of dough can be stored in the refrigerator for 1–2 weeks, if wrapped tightly in plastic. Butter cookie dough can also be frozen. Be sure to wrap well.

Baking parchment saves time and water. Use baking parchment instead of greasing baking sheets.

All cookies can be frozen. They retain optimal flavor for 2–3 months.

"Soft" almond cookies. A piece of soft, white bread in the cookie tin keeps almond cookies soft.

BUTTER COOKIES (basic recipe)
Butter cookie dough with eggs (for rolled cookies)
4 dl (1 ⅔ cups) all-purpose flour
200 g (¾ cup) stick margarine or butter
1 ½ dl (⅔ cup) sugar
1 egg yolk
Butter cookie dough without egg
4 ½ dl (1 ¾ cups) all-purpose flour
1 dl (⅓ cup) sugar
200 g (¾ cup) stick margarine or butter

▶ Combine all ingredients on a work surface, in a mixing bowl or in a food processor.

Flatten the dough, place in a plastic bag and refrigerate for at least 30 minutes. That makes the dough easier to handle.

CHOCOLATE RAISIN DROP COOKIES *approx. 90 cookies*

- Oven temp: *175°C (350°F)*, *convection 175°C (350°F)*

200 g (¾ cup) stick margarine or butter, softened
2 dl (¾ cup) sugar
2 eggs
1 ½ dl (⅔ cup) raisins, chopped
50 g (2 ounces) semi-sweet chocolate, chopped, or 4 tablespoons (¼ cup) semi-sweet chocolate mini-chips
4 tablespoons (¼ cup) diced candied orange peel
6 dl (2 ½ cups) all-purpose flour
1 teaspoon baking powder

▶ Beat the butter and sugar until light and fluffy. Add the eggs, one at a time, beating well after each. Add the fruit and chocolate. Combine the flour and baking powder and stir into the dough. Use two teaspoons to drop spoonfuls of dough onto greased or parchment-lined baking sheets.

Bake on the center oven rack for around 12 minutes.

QUICK OATMEAL COOKIES
approx. 45 cookies

- Oven temp: *175°C (350°F)*, *convection 175°C (350°F)*

3 ½ dl (1 ½ cups) rolled oats
1 ½ dl (⅔ cup) sugar
150 g (⅔ cup) stick margarine or butter

▶ Combine the oats and sugar. Melt the butter and pour over the oat mixture, mixing well. Spoon into mini-muffin tins or into miniature paper cups on a baking sheet.

Bake on the center oven rack for around 10 minutes.

COCONUT CRISP COOKIES
approx. 60 cookies

Very crispy cookies.

- Oven temp: *175°C (350°F)*, *convection 175°C (350°F)*

125 g (½ cup) stick margarine or butter, softened
125 g (½ cup) hydrogenated coconut fat or shortening
3 dl (1 ¼ cups) sugar
1 ½ dl (⅔ cup) potato starch or cornstarch
1 dl (⅓ cup) all-purpose flour
2 teaspoons hornsalt (baking ammonia) or 4 teaspoons baking powder
3 dl (1 ¼ cups) flaked coconut

▶ Beat the butter, coconut fat and sugar until light and fluffy. Combine the dry ingredients and add along with the coconut.

Drop spoonfuls of batter, not too close together, onto greased or parchment-lined baking sheets.

Bake on the center oven rack for around 10 minutes.

Chocolate Raisin Drop Cookies

Quick Oatmeal Cookies

Coconut Crisp Cookies

COCONUT MACAROONS

approx. 35 cookies

- Oven temp: 175°C (350°F),
  convection 175°C (350°F)

50 g (3 tablespoons) stick margarine or
butter, softened

2 eggs

1 ½ dl (⅔ cup) sugar

5–6 dl (2 cups) flaked coconut

▶ Melt the butter and let it cool.

Beat the eggs and sugar until light yellow
and very thick. Add the coconut and butter.
Let the batter rest for a few minutes.

Drop spoonfuls of batter onto greased or
parchment-lined baking sheets.

Bake on the center oven rack for around
12 minutes.

ENGLISH CHRISTMAS
COOKIES *approx. 55 cookies*

These cookies have a fine, piquant flavor.
They are good served year-round, not just at
Christmas time, as their name suggests.

- Oven temp: 175°C (350°F),
  convection 175°C (350°F)

100 g (7 tablespoons) stick margarine or
butter, softened

1 ½ dl (⅔ cup) sugar

1 egg

2 ½ dl (1 cup) all-purpose flour

1 teaspoon baking powder

1/2 teaspoon cinnamon

1 dl (½ cup) chopped nuts

1 dl (⅓ cup) chopped raisins

▶ Beat the butter and sugar until light and
fluffy. Add the egg, beating well. Combine
the flower, baking powder and cinnamon
and add. Fold in the nuts and raisins.

Drop spoonfuls of dough, not too close
together, onto greased or parchment-lined
baking sheets.

Bake on the center oven rack for around 8
minutes.

HAZELNUT DROPS

approx. 40 cookies

Gluten-free cookies

- Oven temp: 200°C (400°F),
  convection 175°C (400°F)

200 g (2 ½ cups) ground hazelnuts

2 dl (1 cup) sugar

1 tablespoon potato starch or cornstarch

2 eggs

whole hazelnuts

▶ Combine all ingredients except for the
whole nuts. With two teaspoons, place
mounds of dough on greased or parchment-
lined baking sheets. Press a whole nut in the
center of each cookie.

Bake on the center oven rack for around 8
minutes. Let cool on the baking sheet.

These cookies are best fresh. Freeze any
that are not eaten the first day.

*English Christmas
Cookies*

Hazelnut Drops

Coconut Macaroons

MERINGUES *approx. 40 cookies*

■ *Oven temp: 125 °C (250 °F), convection 100 °C (210 °F)*

3 egg whites
1 dl (½ cup) sugar

▶ Place the egg whites in a dry, grease-free bowl (important for beating). Add around 1/3 of the sugar and beat until stiff. Fold in the remaining sugar.

Drop, pipe or spread the meringue onto well-greased or parchment-lined baking sheets.

Bake on the center oven rack for around 45 minutes, until dry and light.

ALMOND MERINGUES

approx. 30 cookies

Delicate meringues flavored with almonds and lemon.

■ *Oven temp: 125 °C (250 °F), convection 100 °C (210 °F)*

75 g (¾ cup) flaked almonds
2 egg whites
3 dl (1 ¼ cups) powdered sugar
1 tablespoon lemon juice

▶ Toast the almonds in the oven until pale golden. Let cool.

Beat the egg whites until stiff. Sift over the sugar and continue beating until thick and glossy, around 10 minutes. Beat in the lemon juice by the drop. Fold in the almonds.

Drop onto a greased or parchment-lined baking sheet.

Bake on the center oven rack for around 40 minutes. The meringues should be light and dry, but still a little soft inside.

CARDAMOM MERINGUES

approx. 35 cookies

Serve with ice cream, chocolate mousse or fruit salad.

■ *Oven temp: 100 °C (210 °F), convection 100 °C (210 °F)*

3 egg whites
1 dl (⅓ cup) sugar
1 dl (½ cup) powdered sugar
2 tablespoons cornstarch
¾ teaspoon ground cardamom

▶ Beat the egg whites with half the regular sugar until stiff (preferably with an electric mixer).

Add the remaining sugar, beating until thick and glossy, with no granules left.

Combine the powdered sugar, cornstarch and cardamom and fold into the egg white mixture.

Spoon into a piping bag with a star tip and pipe small kisses or other shapes onto a parchment-lined baking sheet.

Bake on the center oven rack for 45–60 minutes, or until they are very dry and light.

Store in a dry place.

Also pictured on page 79.

MERINGUE RINGS

approx. 25 cookies

■ *Oven temp: 100°C (210°F),*
 convection 100°C (210°F)

3 egg whites
2 dl (¾ cup) sugar
1 dl (⅓ cup) finely chopped nuts (optional)

▶ Pour water into the bottom of a saucepan. Place a bowl, preferably with a round bottom, on top of the saucepan, covering it completely.

Place the egg whites and sugar in the bowl. Heat the water to simmering, beating the egg whites constantly, until the meringue is very stiff and retains its shape.

Fold in the nuts, if desired.

Spoon into a piping bag with a star tip and pipe rings onto a well-greased or parchment-lined baking sheet.

Bake on the center oven rack for around 45 minutes, until the meringues are dry and light.

CALIFORNIA DROPS

approx. 25 cookies

■ *Oven temp: 150°C (300°F),*
 convection 125°C (250°F)

2½ dl (1 cup) dark brown sugar
1 tablespoon cornstarch
¼ teaspoon salt
2 egg whites
2 dl (¾ cup)
 chopped nuts

▶ Combine the brown sugar, cornstarch and salt.

Beat the egg whites until stiff, preferably with an electric mixer.

Carefully stir in the brown sugar mixture. Fold in the nuts.

Drop spoonfuls of batter, not too close together, onto a parchment-lined baking sheet.

Bake on the center oven rack for around 15 minutes. Let cool on the parchment.

Store in an airtight tin.

DREAMS *approx. 50 cookies*

In earlier editions of this book, these cookies were called Sugar Dreams.

- ■ *Oven temp: 150°C (300°F), convection 150°C (300°F)*

100 g (7 tablespoons) stick margarine or butter, softened
3 dl (1 ¼ cups) sugar
2 teaspoons vanilla sugar or 1 teaspoon vanilla extract
1 dl (⅓ cup) corn or safflower oil
1 teaspoon hornsalt (baking ammonia) or 2 teaspoons baking powder
approx. 4 dl (1 ⅔ cups) all-purpose flour
25 almonds, halved

▶ Beat the butter, sugar and vanilla until light and fluffy. Gradually add the oil. Combine the hornsalt with a little flour and beat into the dough. Knead in the remaining flour.

Divide the dough in half. Roll each piece into a rope. Cut each rope into 25 pieces and roll into balls. Place on a greased or parchment-lined baking sheet. Press an almond half into each ball.

Bake on the center oven rack for around 20 minutes.

COCONUT DREAMS
approx. 60 cookies

- ■ *Oven temp: 150°C (300°F), convection 150°C (300°F)*

200 g (¾ cup) stick margarine or butter, softened
1 ½ dl (⅔ cup) sugar
1 teaspoon vanilla sugar or 1/2 teaspoon vanilla extract
2 ½ dl (1 cup) flaked coconut
2 teaspoons hornsalt (baking ammonia) or 4 teaspoons baking powder
approx. 5 dl (2 cups) all-purpose flour

▶ Beat the butter, sugar and vanilla until light and fluffy. Add the remaining ingredients, mixing well. Let the dough rest for around 30 minutes.

Roll the dough into finger-thick ropes. Divide into pieces and roll into balls. Place on a greased or parchment-lined baking sheet.

Bake on the center oven rack for around 15 minutes.

THUMBPRINT COOKIES
approx. 30 cookies

Gluten-free cookies.

- ■ *Oven temp: 175°C (350°F), convection 175°C (350°F)*

125 g (½ cup) stick margarine or butter, softened
½ dl (3 tablespoons) sugar
1 egg yolk

2 ½ dl (1 cup) potato starch or cornstarch

Filling:
½ dl (3–4 tablespoons) thick preserves

▶ Beat the butter and sugar until light and fluffy. Mix in the egg yolk and starch. Roll into small balls.

Place on a greased or parchment-lined baking sheet. Flatten lightly and make a small indentation in the center. Fill with preserves.

Bake on the center oven rack for around 15 minutes.

LILL'S COIN COOKIES
approx. 50 cookies

Gluten-free cookies.

■ *Oven temp: 175 °C (350 °F),*
convection 175 °C (350 °F)

125 g (¼ cup) stick margarine or butter, softened
1 ½ dl (⅔ cup) sugar
2 teaspoons vanilla sugar or 1 teaspoon vanilla extract
1 egg
4 dl (1 ⅔ cups) potato starch or 4 1/2 dl (1 ¾ cups) cornstarch

▶ Beat the butter, sugar and vanilla until light and fluffy. Add the egg and lightly knead in the starch.

Roll into small balls. Place on a greased or parchment-lined baking sheet. Flatten lightly with a fork.

Bake on the center oven rack for 10–15 minutes.

CHOCOLATE MINT TOPS
approx. 60 cookies

☆ This recipe won a prize in 1984.

■ *Oven temp: 175 °C (350 °F),*
convection 175 °C (350 °F)

200 g (¾ cup) stick margarine or butter, softened
1 dl (⅓ cup) powdered sugar
1 dl (⅓ cup) potato starch or (½ cup) cornstarch
4 dl (1 ⅔ cups) all-purpose flour

Glaze:
100 g (3 ounces) semi-sweet chocolate
3–4 drops peppermint oil

▶ Beat the butter and sugar until light and fluffy. Stir in the starch and flour.

Roll into small balls and place on a greased or parchment-lined baking sheet. Make a small indentation in each ball.

Bake on the center oven rack for around 10 minutes. Cool on the baking sheet.

Melt the chocolate in a water bath or microwave oven and stir in the peppermint oil. Fill the indentation with the mint chocolate. Let set.

ALMOND BALLS *approx. 40 cookies*

- *Oven temp: 175°C (350°F),*
  convection 175°C (350°F)

200 g (7 ounces) almond paste

200 g (¾ cup) stick margarine or butter, softened

3 dl (1¼ cups) all-purpose flour

Brushing and garnish:

egg white

sliced almonds

red or green candied
  cherries

▶ Grate the almond paste and mix with the butter until smooth. Knead in the flour. Form into small ropes. Cut into pieces of equal size and roll into balls.

Brush with egg white, roll in almonds and place on a greased or parchment-lined baking sheet. Garnish with halved or quartered cherries.

Bake on the center oven rack for around 10 minutes.

PUNCH BALLS

Follow the recipe for Almond Balls, but add 4 tablespoons (¼ cup) Swedish "Punsch" (arrak-flavored spirits) or anise liqueur and ½–1 dl (⅓ cup) flour to the dough. Roll round balls. Do not use cherries.

VANILLA HORNS *approx. 50 cookies*

- *Oven temp: 175°C (350°F),*
  convection 175°C (350°F)

5 dl (2¼ cups) all-purpose flour

200 g (1 cup) stick margarine or butter

2 tablespoons vanilla sugar or 1 tablespoon
  vanilla extract

sugar

▶ Cut the flour, butter and vanilla together until granular. Knead lightly together. Cover with plastic wrap and refrigerate for at least one hour.

Roll the dough into 8 cm (3 inch) lengths, slightly thicker in the middle. Place on a greased or parchment-lined baking sheet. Bend into horns.

Bake on the center oven rack for around 12 minutes. Dip in sugar while still warm.

NUT HORNS

Follow the recipe for Vanilla Horns but substitute 1 dl (½ cup) ground nuts for 1 dl (½ cup) of the flour. Do not dip the cookies in sugar. Dip the ends in melted chocolate instead.

RICE LOGS *30–40 cookies*

Gluten-free cookies. These can be difficult to roll.

- *Oven temp: 175°C (350°F), convection 175°C (350°F)*

150 g (⅔ cup) stick margarine or butter, softened
¾ dl (⅓ cup) sugar
1 teaspoon vanilla sugar or ½ teaspoon vanilla extract or grated zest of 1 lemon
½ egg
3½ dl (1½ cups) rice flour

Brushing and garnish:
½ egg
4–5 tablespoons pearl sugar

▶ Beat the butter, sugar and vanilla until light and fluffy. Mix in the egg and flour. Wrap in plastic and refrigerate overnight.

Roll finger-thick ropes and cut into 5 cm (2 inch) pieces. Place on a greased or parchment-lined baking sheet.

Brush with beaten egg and sprinkle with pearl sugar.

Bake on the center oven rack for 12–15 minutes.

DESERT SAND COOKIES

approx. 50 cookies

- *Oven temp: 175°C (350°F), convection 175°C (350°F)*

200 g (¾ cup) stick margarine or butter
2 dl (¾ cup) sugar
2 teaspoons vanilla sugar or 1 teaspoon vanilla extract
2 teaspoons baking powder
5 dl (2 cups) all-purpose flour

▶ Brown the butter and let it cool.

Beat the butter, sugar, vanilla and baking powder until light and fluffy. Add the flour and knead lightly together. Form cookies with two teaspoons and place on a greased or parchment-lined baking sheet. Make a groove in each cookie with the side of a spoon.

Bake on the center oven rack for around 15 minutes. Let cool on the baking sheet.

PREACHER'S MOUNDS *60 single or 30 double cookies*

These cookies are similar to Desert Sand Cookies, but they can be sandwiched together with melted chocolate or jelly.

- *Oven temp: 175°C (350°F), convection 175°C (350°F)*

200 g (¾ cup) stick margarine or butter
2 dl (¾ cup) sugar
1 tablespoon vanilla sugar or 1½ teaspoons vanilla extract
5 dl (2 cups) all-purpose flour
1½ teaspoons baking soda

▶ Lightly brown the butter and let it cool.

Beat the butter, sugar and vanilla until light and fluffy. Combine the flour and soda and add, mixing well.

Form cookies with two teaspoons and place on a greased or parchment-lined baking sheet.

Bake on the center oven rack for around 10 minutes.

CURRANT COOKIES

approx. 50 cookies

- Oven temp: 200°C (400°F),
  convection 175°C (350°F)

200 g (¾ cup) stick
  margarine or butter,
  softened

4 tablespoons (¼ cup)
  sugar

2 dl (¾ cup) currants, rinsed
  and dried, if necessary

4½ dl (2 cups) all-purpose flour

▶ Beat the butter and sugar until light and fluffy. Mix in the remaining ingredients. Form into round balls. Place on a greased or parchment-lined baking sheet. Press down with a fork.

Bake on the center oven rack for around 10 minutes.

OAT COOKIES *approx. 50 cookies*

- Oven temp: 200°C (400°F),
  convection 175°C (350°F)

200 g (¾ cup) stick margarine or butter, softened

4 tablespoons (¼ cup) sugar

1½ dl (⅔ cup) rolled oats

3 dl (1¼ cups) all-purpose flour

▶ Beat the butter and sugar until light and fluffy. Mix in the remaining ingredients. Form into round balls. Place on a greased or parchment-lined baking sheet. Press down with a fork.

Bake on the center oven rack for around 10 minutes.

ALMOND LOGS *approx. 18 cookies*

This recipe comes from Denmark.

- Oven temp: 175°C (350°F),
  convection 175°C (350°F)

250 g (9 ounces) almond paste
grated zest of ¼–½ lemon
1 egg white

Glaze:

2 dl (¾ cup) powdered sugar
½ egg white
2 drops vinegar essence

▶ Grate the almond paste and beat until smooth. Add the lemon zest. Whisk the egg white until light peaks form and stir into the almond paste. Pour into a saucepan and place over very low heat. Increase the heat slightly and stir constantly until slightly thickened. Let cool.

Form into 7 cm (2½ inch) long finger-thick ropes. Pinch the tops to make them tri-angular. Place on a greased or parchment-lined baking sheet.

Bake on the center oven rack until they are light brown but still soft inside, around 10 minutes.

Let cool completely.

For the glaze, beat the sugar and egg white until thick and smooth. Add the vinegar.

Make a small paper cone, fill with the egg white mixture and cut a tiny hole in the tip. Drizzle the glaze in a zig-zag over the cookies.

TIVOLI BARS *approx. 20 cookies*

■ *Oven temp: 200°C (400°F), 175°C (350°F)*

Butter cookie base:

125 g (½ cup) stick margarine or butter, softened

½ dl (3 tablespoons) sugar

1 egg yolk

3 dl (1 ¼ dl) all-purpose flour

Filling:

50 g (4 tablespoons) stick margarine or butter, softened

1 dl (½ cup) sugar

1 medium boiled potato (around 85 g/3 ounces)

50 g (½ cup) finely chopped almonds

1 egg white

Glaze:

2 dl (¾ cup) powdered sugar

1 ½ tablespoons water

50 g (3 tablespoons) chopped candied orange peel

▶ Grease or line a 25 cm (10 inch) square or 20 × 30 cm (8 × 12 inch) pan with baking parchment.

Beat the butter and sugar until light and fluffy. Add the egg yolk and flour, kneading lightly. Wrap in plastic and refrigerate for at least 30 minutes.

For the filling, beat the butter and sugar until light and fluffy. Mash the potato and add with the almonds. Beat the egg whites until stiff and fold into the almond mixture.

Press the cookie base evenly into the pan. Spread the filling over the base.

Bake on the center oven rack for around 15 minutes. Let cool.

For the glaze, beat the sugar and water until thick. Spread over the cookies and sprinkle with peel. Let set for a few minutes, then cut into diamonds.

ALMOND SPICE COOKIES

approx. 75 cookies

■ *Oven temp: 200°C (400°F), convection 175°C (350°F)*

200 g (¾ cup) stick margarine or butter, softened

2 dl (¾ cup) sugar

1 egg

5 ½ dl (2 ¼ cups) all-purpose flour

2 teaspoons baking powder

1 teaspoon cinnamon

1 teaspoon ground cardamom

75 g (⅔ cup) ground almonds

Garnish:

pearl sugar

▶ Beat the butter and sugar until light and fluffy. Beat in the egg. Combine the remaining ingredients and add, kneading lightly.

Form into small balls. Dip in pearl sugar and place on a greased or parchment-lined baking sheet.

Bake on the center oven rack for 10–12 minutes.

STENHAMMAR COOKIES
approx. 85 cookies

■ *Oven temp: 175°C (350°F),*
   convection 175°C (350°F)
300 g (1 ¼ cups) stick margarine or butter,
   softened
7 ½ dl (3 cups) all-purpose flour
3 dl (1 ¼ cups) sugar
1 teaspoon baking powder
1 ½ dl (⅔ cup) currants
1 dl (½ cup) ground almonds
Brushing and garnish:
1 egg, lightly beaten
chopped
   almonds

▶ Combine all the ingredients, kneading lightly. Divide into 6 pieces and roll into finger-thick ropes.

Place on a greased or parchment-lined baking sheet. Flatten slightly. Brush with beaten egg and sprinkle with chopped almonds.

Bake on the center oven rack for around 15 minutes.

Cut into 2 cm (¾ inch) wide diagonal slices while still warm.

JELLY SLICES *approx. 60 cookies*
☆ This recipe won a prize in 1945.

■ *Oven temp: 200°C (400°F),*
   convection 175°C (350°F)
250 g (1 cup) stick margarine or butter,
   softened
1 ½ dl (⅔ cup) sugar
2 eggs
6 dl (2 ½ cups) all-purpose flour
1 teaspoon baking powder
Filling:
3–4 tablespoons thick red fruit preserves
Glaze:
2 dl (¾ cup) powdered sugar
1 ½ tablespoons water

▶ Beat the butter and sugar until light and fluffy. Beat in the eggs, one at a time, beating well after each. Combine the dry ingredients and add, mixing well.

Divide into 4 pieces. Roll each into a 40 cm (16 inch) length. Place on greased or parchment-lined baking sheets. Make an indentation along the center of each length and fill with preserves.

Bake on the center oven rack for around 15 minutes.

For the glaze, combine the sugar and water and spread over the warm cookies. Cut into 2 cm (¾ inch) wide diagonal slices while still warm.

APPLE SLICES *approx. 30 cookies*

☆ This recipe won a prize in 1945.

■ *Oven temp: 200°C (400°F),*
  convection 175°C (350°F)

2½ dl (1 cup) flour
100 g (7 tablespoons) stick margarine or butter, softened
3 tablespoons sugar
1 tablespoon light cream

Filling:
1 dl (½ cup) thick applesauce

▶ Combine all the ingredients, mixing well. Wrap in plastic and refrigerate for a couple of hours.

Roll into two 30 cm (12 inches) lengths. Place on a greased or parchment-lined baking sheet.

Make an indentation along the center of each length and fill with applesauce.

Bake on the center oven rack for 10–12 minutes

Cut into 2 cm (¾ inch) wide diagonal slices while still warm.

Also pictured on page 79.

FINNISH LOGS *approx. 50 cookies*

■ *Oven temp: 175°C (350°F), 175°C (350°F)*

50 g (½ cup) ground almonds
¼ teaspoon almond extract
4½ dl (2 cups) all-purpose flour
1 dl (½ cup) sugar
200 g (1 cup) stick margarine or butter

Brushing and garnish:
½–1 egg white, lightly beaten
pearl sugar
chopped almonds

▶ Combine the dry ingredients and cut in the butter, kneading lightly. Wrap in plastic and refrigerate for around an hour.

Roll into finger-thick ropes and cut into 4–5 cm (2 inch) pieces. Place close together on a greased or parchment-lined baking sheet. Brush with egg white and sprinkle with pearl sugar and chopped almonds.

Bake on the center oven rack for around 12 minutes.

LEMON LOGS *approx. 30 cookies*

■ *Oven temp: 200°C (400°F),*
  convection 175°C (350°F)

2½ dl (1 cup) all-purpose flour
1 dl (⅓ cup) sugar
½ teaspoon baking powder
grated zest of 1 lemon
75 g (5 tablespoons) stick margarine or butter
1 small egg

Brushing:
1 egg, lightly beaten

▶ Combine the dry ingredients and cut in the butter, kneading lightly. Wrap in plastic and refrigerate for around an hour.

Roll into finger-thick ropes and cut into 5 cm (2 inch) pieces. Place on a greased or parchment-lined baking sheet. Brush with beaten egg.

Bake on the center oven rack for around 8 minutes.

RYE LOGS *approx. 50 cookies*

A simple, everyday cookie with a rich rye flavor.

- *Oven temp: 175°C (350°F), convection 175°C (350°F)*

3 dl (1 ⅓ cups) all-purpose flour
1 dl (⅓ cup) coarse rye flour
150 g (⅔ cup) margarine, softened
1 dl (½ cup) sugar
1 teaspoon vanilla sugar or ½ teaspoon vanilla

▶ Combine all the ingredients, mixing well. Roll into finger-thick ropes and cut into 5 cm (2 inch) pieces. Place on a greased or parchment-lined baking sheet. Press each down lightly with a fork.

Bake on the center oven rack for around 12 minutes.

Pictured on page 79.

CHOCOLATE CIGARS

around 75 cookies

- *Oven temp: 175°C (350°F), convection 175°C (350°F)*

175 g (¾ cup) stick margarine or butter, softened
1 dl (⅓ cup) sugar
125 g (1 cup) ground walnuts
3 dl (1 ¼ cups) all-purpose flour
2 tablespoons milk or light cream

Garnish:
50 g (2 ounces) semi-sweet chocolate

▶ Beat the butter and sugar until light and fluffy. Stir in the nuts and flour, then the milk.

Roll into small finger-thick ropes and cut into 5 cm (2 inch) pieces. Place on a greased or parchment-lined baking sheet.

Bake on the center oven rack for around 12 minutes.

Melt the chocolate in a water bath or in a microwave oven, see page 122. Dip one end of each cookie in the chocolate.

MARTA'S CHOCOLATE SLICES

around 60 cookies

- *Oven temp: 200°C (400°F), convection 175°C (350°F)*

200 g (¾ cup) stick margarine or butter, softened
2 ½ dl (1 cup) sugar
5 dl (2 cups) all-purpose flour
4 tablespoons (¼ cup) cocoa
1 teaspoon baking powder
1 ½ teaspoons vanilla
1 egg

Brushing and garnish:
1 egg, lightly beaten
pearl sugar

▶ Combine all the ingredients, mixing well.

Divide into 6 pieces. Form into logs. Place on greased or parchment-lined baking sheets. Flatten slightly. Brush with beaten egg and sprinkle with pearl sugar.

Bake on the center oven rack for around 15 minutes.

Cut into 2 cm (¾ inch) wide diagonal slices while still warm.

Pictured at right: Marta's Chocolate Slices.

HORSESHOES *approx. 50 cookies*

■ *Oven temp: 225 °C (425 °F), 200 °C (400 °F)*
5 dl (2 cups) all-purpose flour
2 dl (¾ cup) sugar
200 g (¾ cup) stick margarine or butter
1 ½ tablespoons molasses
1 teaspoon ground cardamom
2 teaspoons cinnamon
2 teaspoons baking soda stirred into 1 tea-
    spoon warm water

▶ Combine all the ingredients, mixing well.
Roll out into narrow ropes. Cut into 7–8
cm (3 inch) pieces and form into horseshoes.
Place on a greased or parchment-lined baking sheet. Press down with a fork.
Bake on the center oven rack for around 7
minutes.

NUTMEG SLICES *approx. 40 cookies*

■ *Oven temp: 175 °C (350 °F),*
    convection 175 °C (350 °F)
250 g (1 cup) stick margarine or butter,
    softened
1 ½ dl (⅔ cup) sugar
1 tablespoon cinnamon
½ teaspoon grated nutmeg
5 dl (2 cups) all-purpose flour

▶ Beat the butter, sugar and spices until
light and fluffy. Add the flour, kneading
lightly.

Divide into 4 pieces. Form each into a 40
cm (16 inch) log. Place on greased or parchment-lined baking sheets. Press down lightly with a fork to make stripes in the dough.
Bake on the center oven rack for around
20 minutes.
Cut each length into 10 diagonal slices
while still warm.

CHECKERBOARD COOKIES
approx. 50 cookies

■ *Oven temp: 200 °C (400 °F),*
    convection 175 °C (350 °F)
4 ½–5 dl (2 cups) all-purpose flour
1 dl (⅓ cup) sugar
200 g (¾ cup) stick margarine or butter
Flavoring:
2 teaspoons vanilla sugar or
    1 teaspoon vanilla extract
2 tablespoons cocoa

▶ Combine the flour and
sugar and cut in the butter,
kneading lightly. Divide in half.
Add the vanilla to one half, the cocoa to the
other.
Roll each half into two ropes. Place a dark
and light together, then a light and dark on
top. Press lightly together. Wrap in plastic
and refrigerate for at least an hour. Cut into
3–4 mm (¼ inch) slices. Place on a greased or
parchment-lined baking sheet.
Bake on the center oven rack for around
10 minutes.

CHOCOLATE SWIRLS
around 75 cookies

Follow the recipe for Checkerboard Cookies, but roll each half into a 15 × 40 cm
(6 × 16 inch) sheet. Place the dark sheet on
the light and roll lengthwise. Wrap in plastic and refrigerate for at least an hour. Cut
into 3–4 mm (¼ inch) slices. Place on a
greased or parchment-lined baking sheet.
Bake on the center oven rack for around 6
minutes. Pictured on page 79.

STINA'S COOKIES *approx. 60 cookies*

☆ This recipe won a prize in 1984.

■ *Oven temp: 200°C (400°F),*
convection 175°C (350°F)

200 g (¾ cup) stick margarine or butter, softened

1 ½ dl (⅔ cup) powdered sugar

50 g (2 ounces) almond paste

½ teaspoon vanilla

grated zest of ½ lemon

3 ½ dl (1 ½ cups) all-purpose flour

Brushing and garnish:

1 egg, lightly beaten

½ dl (3 tablespoons) sugar

▶ Beat the butter and sugar until light and fluffy. Grate the almond paste and add with the vanilla and lemon zest. Knead in the flour. Form into two 3 cm (1 ¼ inch) thick ropes. Wrap in plastic and refrigerate for at least one hour.

Brush the ropes with beaten egg and roll in sugar. Cut into ½ cm (¼ inch) slices. Place on a greased or parchment-lined baking sheet.

Bake on the center oven rack for around 10 minutes.

BRUSSELS COOKIES

approx. 50 cookies

■ *Oven temp: 175°C (350°F),*
convection 175°C (350°F)

4 ½–5 dl (2 cups) all-purpose flour

1 dl (½ cup) sugar

2 teaspoons vanilla sugar or 1 teaspoon vanilla extract

200 g (¾ cup) stick margarine or butter

Garnish:

pearl or regular sugar

▶ Combine the dry ingredients and cut in the butter, kneading lightly.

Form into 4 cm (1 ½ inches) thick ropes and roll in sugar. Wrap in plastic and refrigerate for at least one hour. Cut into slices. Place on a greased or parchment-lined baking sheet.

Bake on the center oven rack for around 10 minutes.

JAM-FILLED BRUSSELS COOKIES *approx. 50 cookies*

Prepare the recipe for Brussels Cookies, but roll in pearl sugar and chopped almonds and slice. Make a dip in the center of each and fill with jam. Bake.

FARMERS' COOKIES

approx. 70 cookies

- *Oven temp: 200°C (400°F), convection 175°C (350°F)*

5 ½ dl (2 ¼ cups) all-purpose flour
2 dl (¾ cup) sugar
1 tablespoon light molasses or corn syrup
1 teaspoon baking soda
1 tablespoon water
¾ dl (⅓ cup) chopped almonds
200 g (¾ cup) stick margarine or butter, sliced

▶ Make a mound of flour on a work surface. Add the remaining ingredients. Quickly cut in the butter, kneading lightly.

Form into two logs, 4–5 cm (2 inches) thick. Wrap in plastic and refrigerate for at least two hours, until hard.

Cut into ½ cm (¼ inch) slices. Place on a greased or parchment-lined baking sheet.

Bake on the center oven rack for 5–7 minutes, until golden.

SONJA'S AMERICAN COOKIES

approx. 120 cookies

- *Oven temp: 200°C (400°F), convection 175°C (350°F)*

250 g (1 cup) stick margarine or butter, softened
2 dl (¾ cup) sugar
1 egg
1 tablespoon dark corn syrup
½ teaspoon vanilla
¾ dl (⅓ cup) chopped almonds or walnuts
½ teaspoon baking powder
5 ½ dl (2 ¼ cups) all-purpose flour

▶ Beat the butter and sugar until light and fluffy. Add the egg, syrup, vanilla and nuts, mixing well. Combine the dry ingredients and add, kneading lightly. Form into rolls, around 4 cm (1 ½ inches) thick. Refrigerate overnight.

Cut into thin slices and place on greased or parchment-lined baking sheets.

Bake on the center oven rack for around 5 minutes.

ELSA'S RYE COOKIES
approx. 60 cookies
- Oven temp: 175 °C (350 °F),
  convection 175 °C (350 °F)

1 ½ dl (⅔ cup) all-purpose flour
½ teaspoon salt
1 teaspoon ginger
1 teaspoon cinnamon
2 teaspoons baking powder
¾ dl (⅓ cup) sugar
200 g (¾ cup) stick margarine or butter
2 tablespoons honey
1 egg
3 ¾ dl (1 ½ cups) fine rye flour

▶ Combine the flour, salt, ginger, cinnamon, baking powder and sugar. Cut in the butter. Add the remaining ingredients, kneading lightly. Form into two 3 cm (1 ¼ inches) thick rolls. Wrap in plastic and refrigerate for a couple of hours.

Cut into 1 cm (⅜ inch) slices. Place on a greased or parchment-lined baking sheet.

Bake on the center oven rack for around 10 minutes.

SONJA'S NUT COOKIES
approx. 90 cookies
- Oven temp: 200 °C (400 °F),
  convection 175 °C (350 °F)

200 g (¾ cup) stick margarine or butter, softened
1 dl (½ cup) sugar
200 g (2 ½ cups) ground hazelnuts
3 ½–4 dl (1 ½–1 ⅔ cups) all-purpose flour
Filling:
40–75 g (1 ½–3 ounces) semi-sweet chocolate

▶ Beat the butter and sugar until light and fluffy. Add the remaining ingredients, mixing well. Form into 2 cm (¾ inch) thick rolls. Wrap in plastic and refrigerate for several hours, preferably overnight.

Cut into ½ cm (¼ inch) slices. Place on a greased or parchment-lined baking sheet.

Bake on the center oven rack for around 5 minutes.

Chop the chocolate and melt in a water bath or in the microwave oven, see page 122. Sandwich the cookies with melted chocolate.

GINGER COOKIES *approx. 45 cookies*

☆ This recipe won a prize in 1975.

■ *Oven temp: 200 °C (400 °F),*
convection 175 °C (350 °F)

150 g (⅔ cup) stick margarine or butter, softened
¾ dl (⅓ cup) sugar
2 tablespoons chopped candied ginger
½ teaspoon ground ginger
4 dl (1 ⅔ cups) all-purpose flour

▶ Beat the butter and sugar until light and fluffy. Add the remaining ingredients, kneading until smooth. Wrap in plastic and refrigerate for around one hour.

Using a fork, press into a 25 × 35 cm (10 × 14 inch) layer on a greased baking sheet.

Bake on the center oven rack for around 13 minutes.

Cut into triangles while still warm. Let cool on the baking sheet.

Variation: Form the dough into lengths and flatten with a fork. Bake. Cut into diagonal slices.

Almond Jitterbugs

JITTERBUGS *approx. 50 cookies*

■ *Oven temp: 175 °C (350 °F),*
convection 175 °C (350 °F)

Butter cookie dough:
4 ½ dl (2 cups) all-purpose flour
1 dl (½ cup) sugar
200 g (¾ cup) stick margarine or butter
1 egg yolk

Filling:
1–2 egg whites
1 dl (⅓–½ cup) sugar

▶ Combine the dry ingredients and cut in the butter. Add the egg yolk, mixing well. Wrap in plastic and refrigerate for at least 30 minutes.

Beat the egg whites until stiff. Beat in the sugar until thick and glossy.

Divide the dough in half. Roll each into a ½ cm (¼ inch) rectangle, 16 × 30 cm (6 × 12 inches). Spread half the filling on each and roll up like jelly rolls. Place on a cutting board and refrigerate for at least 30 minutes. Cut into 1 cm (⅜ inch) slices. Place on a greased or parchment-lined baking sheet.

Bake on the center oven rack for 12–15 minutes.

ALMOND JITTERBUGS
approx. 35 cookies

■ *Oven temp: 175 °C (350 °F),*
convection 175 °C (350 °F)

1 batch butter cookie dough for Jitterbugs
Filling:
200 g (7 ounces) almond paste
2 egg whites

▶ Prepare the butter cookie dough. Grate the almond paste and mix with the egg whites, preferably in a food processor. Follow the recipe for Jitterbugs with the almond filling but cut into slightly thicker slices.

CHOCOLATE NUT BARS

approx. 40 cookies

■ *Oven temp: 200 °C (400 °F),*
  convection 175 °C (350 °F)

Butter cookie dough:
3 ¼ dl (1 ⅓ cups) all-purpose flour
1 dl (⅓ cup) sugar
125 g (½ cup) stick margarine or butter
1 egg yolk

Almond filling:
2 tablespoons stick margarine or butter
1 dl (½ cup) sugar
65 g (⅔ cup) ground almonds
1 cold boiled potato (50 g/2 ounces), peeled
  and mashed
1 egg white

Garnish:
200 g (1 small package/6 ounces) semi-
  sweet chocolate chips
½ dl (¼ cup) chopped toasted almonds

▶ Combine the dry ingredients and cut in the butter. Add the egg yolk, mixing well. Wrap in plastic and let the dough rest for at least an hour.

Beat the butter and sugar until light and fluffy. Add the nuts and potato. Whisk the egg white lightly and add, mixing to combine.

Roll the dough into a rectangle and place on a greased or parchment-lined baking sheet. Spread the almond mixture over the dough.

Bake on a lower oven rack for around 10 minutes.

Remove the cake from the oven and immediately sprinkle with chocolate chips. When the chips are melted, spread the chocolate all over the cookies. Sprinkle with almonds.

When completely cold, cut into squares.

CHOCOLATE NUT BARS *approx. 30 cookies*

■ *Oven temp: 200 °C (400 °F),*
  convection 175 °C (350 °F)
100 g (7 tablespoons) stick margarine or
  butter, softened
1 ¼ dl (⅔ cup) sugar
1 teaspoon vanilla sugar or ½ teaspoon
  vanilla extract
1 egg
1 ¼ dl (½ cup) all-purpose flour
½ teaspoon baking powder
2 tablespoons cocoa

Garnish:
100 g (¾ cup) coarsely chopped walnuts or
  almonds

▶ Grease or line a 25 × 35 cm (10 × 14 inch) pan with baking parchment.

Beat the butter, sugar, vanilla and egg until light and fluffy. Combine the dry ingredients and add, mixing well.

Pour into the prepared pan. Sprinkle with nuts. Bake on the center oven rack for 15 minutes.

Cut into 5 cm (2 inch) squares while still warm.

COGNAC WREATHS

approx. 50 cookies

■ *Oven temp: 200 °C (400 °F), convection 175 °C (350 °F)*

5 dl (2 cups) all-purpose flour
I dl (½ cup) sugar
200 g (¾ cup) stick margarine or butter
2 tablespoons cognac

▶ Combine the dry ingredients and cut in the butter. Add the cognac, kneading until smooth. Wrap in plastic and refrigerate for at least an hour.

Cut the dough into pieces. Roll into very narrow lengths. Twist two lengths together, then cut into 12 cm (5 inch) pieces. Form into wreaths and place, seam side down, on a greased or parchment-lined baking sheet.

Bake on the center oven rack for around 10 minutes.

LEKEBERG WREATHS

approx. 65 cookies

■ *Oven temp: 175 °C (350 °F), convection 175 °C (350 °F)*

225 g (1 cup) stick margarine or butter, softened
1 ½ dl (⅔ cup) sugar
I dl (½ cup) cocoa, sifted
2 egg yolks
4 ½ dl (2 cups) all-purpose flour
Garnish:
powdered sugar

▶ Beat the butter, sugar and cocoa until light and fluffy. Add the egg yolks, one at a time, beating well after each. Gradually add the flour, kneading lightly.

Using a cookie press or pastry bag with a small star tip, pipe 10 cm (4 inch) lengths. Form into wreaths and place on a greased or parchment-lined baking sheet.

Bake on the center oven rack for 10–13 minutes.

Let the cookies mature for a few days. Sift powdered sugar over right before serving.

SUGAR PRETZELS *approx. 50 cookies*

These are also called Glass Wreaths or Glass Pretzels.

■ *Oven temp: 225 °C (425 °F), convection 200 °C (400 °F)*

125 g (½ cup) stick margarine or butter

2 dl (1 cup) all-purpose flour
2 tablespoons light cream
Garnish:
sugar

▶ Cut the butter into the flour. Add the cream and mix quickly together. Wrap in plastic and refrigerate for several hours.

Roll into a ½ cm (¼ inch) thick, 15 cm (6 inch) wide rectangle. Cut horizontally into 1 cm (⅜ inch) wide strips.

Form into pretzels, as illustrated, and place on a greased or parchment-lined baking sheet.

Bake on the center oven rack for around 7 minutes.

Remove from the oven and immediately dip in sugar to coat all sides.

BUTTER WREATHS *approx. 20 cookies*

These cookies are sugar-free.

- *Oven temp: 250°C (450°F), convection 225°C (425°F)*

2½ dl (1 cup) flour
150 g (⅔ cup) cold
    stick margarine
    or butter
2 tablespoons
    cold water

Brushing:
beaten egg

▶ Make a mound of flour on a work surface. Dice the butter and cut into the flour. Add the water and toss quickly together. Do not knead. Cover with plastic and refrigerate for around an hour.

Roll into a ½ cm (¼ inch) thick sheet on a floured surface. Cut out cookies with a wreath or posy cookie cutter and place on a rinsed or parchment-lined baking sheet. Brush with beaten egg.

Bake on the center oven rack for around 6 minutes.

KARL XV'S WREATHS

approx. 30 cookies

- *Oven temp: 200°C (400°F), convection 175°C (350°F)*

150 g (⅔ cup) stick margarine or butter
4 tablespoons (¼ cup) whipping cream
4 dl (1⅔ cups) all-purpose flour

Brushing and garnish:
water, pearl sugar

▶ Beat the butter until fluffy. Add the remaining ingredients, mixing well. Roll into narrow lengths, around 20 cm (8 inches) long. Form into pretzels or wreaths. Brush with water and dip in pearl sugar. Place on a greased or parchment-lined baking sheet. Press down to flatten.

Bake on the center oven rack for around 12 minutes.

EGG PRETZELS *approx. 45 cookies*

- *Oven temp: 200°C (400°F), convection 175°C (350°F)*

2 boiled egg yolks
2 raw egg yolks
150 g (⅔ cup) stick margarine or butter, softened
1 dl (½ cup) sugar
4–5 dl (1¾–2 cups) all-purpose flour

Brushing and garnish:
beaten egg white
pearl sugar

▶ Press the boiled yolks through a sieve or mash well. Mix in the raw yolks. Beat the butter, sugar and egg yolks until light and fluffy. Add the sugar, mixing well.

Roll the dough into narrow ropes. Form into pretzels or wreaths and place on a greased or parchment-lined baking sheet. Brush with beaten egg white and sprinkle with pearl sugar.

Bake on the center oven rack for 7–8 minutes.

Karl XV's Pretzels

Egg Pretzels

POTATO PRETZELS

approx. 30 cookies

- Oven temp: 175°C (350°F),
  convection 175°C (350°F)

100 g (7 tablespoons) stick margarine or butter, softened
1 ½ dl (⅔ cup) grated cold boiled potato

2 ½ dl (1 cup) all-purpose flour
½ teaspoon baking powder
⅛ teaspoon almond extract, optional
Garnish:
pearl sugar

▶ Beat the butter until light and fluffy. Add the remaining ingredients, mixing quickly together.

Roll the dough into narrow ropes. Cut into 15 cm (6 inch) lengths. Form into wreaths and dip in pearl sugar. Place on a greased or parchment-lined baking sheet.

Bake on the center oven rack for around 10 minutes.

BONNA WREATHS *approx. 30 cookies*

These are good when spread with butter or honey.

- Oven temp: 225°C (425°F),
  convection 200°C (400°F)

2 tablespoons sugar
½ teaspoon salt
1 tablespoon hornsalt (baking ammonia) or 2 tablespoons baking powder
8 dl (3 ⅓ cups) rye flour (or half rye, half all-purpose)
100 g (7 tablespoons) lard or 125 g (½ cup) margarine
3 dl (1 ¼ cups) sour cream

▶ Combine the dry ingredients. Add the lard and sour cream, kneading well. The dough should be rather stiff.

Divide into 30 pieces and roll each into a 20 cm (8 inch) rope. Form into wreaths and place on a greased or parchment-lined baking sheet.

Bake on the center oven rack for around 8 minutes.

Pictured at right from the left: Marstrand Cookies, page 113; Aja Cookies, page 106; and Grandmother's Spritz Wreaths, page 106

STRASSBURGERS *approx. 25 cookies*

- *Oven temp: 175°C (350°F), convection 175°C (350°F)*

100 g (7 tablespoons) stick margarine or butter, softened
½ dl (¼ cup) powdered sugar
1 tablespoon vanilla sugar or 1 ½ teaspoons vanilla extract
1 ¼ dl (⅔ cup) all-purpose flour
1 dl (⅓ cup) potato starch or cornstarch
Garnish:
powdered jelly or sugar
melted semi-sweet chocolate, see page 122

▶ Beat the butter, sugar and vanilla until light and fluffy. Gradually add the flour and starch, mixing well.

Using a cookie press or bag with a star tip, make mounds or lengths directly onto a greased or parchment-lined baking sheet.

Bake on the center oven rack for around 10 minutes.

Pipe a little jelly onto each cookie or sift powdered sugar over and dip one end in melted chocolate. Pictured on page 79.

AJA COOKIES *approx. 25 cookies*

- *Oven temp: 175°C (350°F), convection 175°C (350°F)*

3 ½ dl (1 ½ cups) all-purpose flour
1 dl (⅓ cup) potato starch
¾ dl (⅓ cup) powdered sugar
200 g (¾ cup) stick margarine or butter
Filling: thick applesauce, jelly or chocolate
Garnish: powdered sugar

▶ Combine the dry ingredients and cut in the butter, mixing well.

Using a cookie press or bag with a star tip, make small flat rosettes directly onto a greased or parchment-lined baking sheet.

Bake on the center oven rack for around 10 minutes.

Sandwich two cookies together with applesauce, jelly or melted chocolate in between. Sift a little powdered sugar over the cookies just before serving.

Pictured on page 105.

GRANDMOTHER'S SPRITZ WREATHS *approx. 60 cookies*

Tender, crisp, delicate cookies.

- *Oven temp: 200°C (400°F), convection 175°C (350°F)*

200 g (¾ cup) stick margarine or butter, softened
2 dl (¾ cup) powdered sugar
65 g (⅔ cup) ground almonds
1 egg yolk
4 dl (1 ⅔ cups) all-purpose flour

▶ Beat the butter and sugar until light and fluffy. Add the remaining ingredients, mixing well.

Using a cookie press or pastry bag with a star tip, press out long strips. Cut into 8 cm (3 inch) pieces. Form into wreaths. Place on a greased or parchment-lined baking sheet.

Bake on the center oven rack for around 8 minutes. Pictured on page 105.

HORSESHOES WITH STUDS *approx. 60 cookies*

- *Oven temp: 200°C (400°F), convection 175°C (350°F)*

300 g (10 ounces) almond paste
100 g (7 tablespoons) stick margarine or butter
2 ¼ dl (1 cup) all-purpose flour
Garnish:
powdered sugar
beaten egg white
semi-sweet chocolate mini-chips

▶ Coarsely grate the almond paste. Beat in the butter and flour. Knead until smooth.

Using a cookie press or pastry bag, press out long strips and cut into 10 cm (4 inch) pieces. Form into horseshoes on a greased or parchment-lined baking sheet.

Bake on the center oven rack for around 8 minutes.

Let cool completely.

Garnish with powdered sugar mixed with a little egg white and chocolate mini-chips.

MOCHA NESTS *approx. 50 cookies*

You need a potato ricer to make these cookies.

■ *Oven temp: 175 °C (350 °F),*
  convection 175 °C (350 °F)
200 g (¾ cup) stick margarine or butter
3¾ dl (1½ cups) all-purpose flour
1¼ dl (½ cup) potato starch or cornstarch
1 dl (½ cup) sugar
1 tablespoon cocoa
1½ teaspoons vanilla sugar or 1 teaspoon
  vanilla extract
2 teaspoons instant coffee granules + 1 tablespoon water

▶ Dice the butter and cut it into the dry ingredients. Add the coffee, kneading well. Wrap in plastic and refrigerate or at least an hour.

Press through a potato ricer.

Using two teaspoons, make small mounds of dough on a greased or parchment-lined baking sheet.

Bake on the center oven rack for around 12 minutes.

ALMOND MACAROONS
approx. 25 cookies

These small elegant cookies are also called Tea Cookies.

■ *Oven temp: 200 °C (400 °F),*
  convection 175 °C (350 °F)
100 g (1 cup) finely ground almonds
1½ dl (⅔ cup) powdered sugar
½–1 egg white
red or green food coloring (optional)
Garnish:
hazelnuts, candied orange peel, candied cherries
melted semi-sweet
  chocolate
  (optional)

▶ Combine the almonds and sugar. Gradually add the egg white, kneading well. The mixture should be smooth but also loose enough to be pressed through a piping bag. Tint the dough, if desired.

Form into balls or logs or make small rosettes with a star tip. Garnish with nuts, peel or cherries. Place on greased or parchment-lined baking sheets.

Bake on the center oven rack for around 8 minutes.

Let the cookies cool completely. Dip in melted chocolate, if desired, see page 122.

Note: 200 g (7 ounces) almond paste and 1 egg white may be substituted for the above ingredients.

MARGIT'S HEARTS *40–50 cookies*

☆ This recipe won a prize in 1984.

- Oven temp: 200°C (400°F),
  convection 175°C (350°F)

1 dl (½ cup) powdered sugar
4 dl (1 ⅔ cups) all-purpose flour
1 dl (⅓ cup) cornstarch
200 g (¾ cup) stick margarine or butter
2 tablespoons light molasses or light corn
  syrup
1 teaspoon vanilla sugar or ½ teaspoon
  vanilla extract

▶ Combine the dry ingredients. Cut in the butter until crumbly. Add the molasses and vanilla, mixing quickly together.

Press a thin layer of dough into greased individual heart-shaped tins. Place the tins on a baking sheet.

Bake on the center oven rack for around 7 minutes. Let cool slightly, then carefully tap out of the tins.

These can be filled with whipped cream and fruit for dessert.

Coconut Shells

OAT BASKETS *approx. 40 cookies*

- Oven temp: 200°C (400°F),
  convection 175°C (350°F)

200 g (¾ cup) stick margarine or butter,
  softened
1 ½ dl (⅔ cup) sugar
3 ½ dl (1 ½ cups) all-purpose flour
3 dl (1 ¼ cups)
  rolled oats
¼ teaspoon
  almond
  extract

▶ Beat the butter and sugar until light and fluffy. Add the remaining ingredients, mixing well. Press a layer of dough into greased individual baking tins. Place the tins on a baking sheet.

Bake on the center oven rack for around 10 minutes.

Let cool completely, then carefully tap out of the tins.

COCONUT SHELLS
approx. 50 cookies

- Oven temp: 200°C (400°F),
  convection 175°C (350°F)

1 dl (½ cup) flaked coconut
200 g (¾ cup) stick margarine or butter,
  softened
1 dl (⅓ cup) sugar
½ egg
5 dl (2 cups) all-purpose flour

▶ Toast the coconut in the oven until light golden.

Beat the butter and sugar until light and fluffy. Add the remaining ingredients, mixing well. Cover and refrigerate for at least an hour.

Press a layer of dough into greased individual baking tins. Place the tins on a baking sheet.

Bake on the center oven rack for around 8 minutes.

Let cool slightly, then carefully tap out of the tins.

BIRGITS ALMOND SHELLS

approx. 50 cookies

- Oven temp. 200 °C (400 °F),
  convection 175 °C (350 °F)

200 g (¾ cup) stick margarine or butter, softened

1 ½ dl (⅔ cup) sugar

125 g (1 cup) ground almonds

¼ teaspoon almond extract

1 egg

4 dl (1 ⅔ cups) all-purpose flour

▶ Beat the butter and sugar until light and fluffy. Add the remaining ingredients, reserving a little of the flour. Knead the dough lightly, adding the remaining flour. Cover with plastic and refrigerate for at least an hour.

Form the dough into a narrow log. Cut into pieces and press into greased individual baking tins. Place the tins on a baking sheet.

Bake on the center oven rack for around 8 minutes.

Tap out of the tins immediately.

SUGAR-FREE ALMOND SHELLS

approx. 25 shells

- Oven temp: 250 °C (450 °F),
  convection 225 °C (425 °F)

75 g (⅔ cup) ground almonds

3 ½ dl (1 ½ cups) all-purpose flour

150 g (⅔ cup) cold stick margarine or butter

½ egg

⅛ teaspoon almond extract

▶ Combine the almonds and flour. Dice the butter and cut into the almond mixture. Whisk in the egg and extract, mixing well. Form into a log, wrap in plastic and refrigerate for 30 minutes.

Cut the log into 25 pieces and press each into a lightly greased individual baking tin. Place the tins on a baking sheet.

Bake on a lower oven rack for 8–10 minutes. Let cool slightly, then carefully tap out of the tins onto a rack.

Serve filled with whipped cream and berries.

GINGER LACE COOKIES

approx. 20 cookies

Crispy, easy to bake cookies that keep well.

- *Oven temp: 200°C (400°F), convection 175°C (350°F)*

50 g (3 tablespoons) stick margarine or butter, softened
½ dl (3 tablespoons) sugar
½ teaspoon ginger
¼ teaspoon vanilla
¾ dl (⅓ cup) all-purpose flour

▶ Beat the butter, sugar, ginger and vanilla until light and fluffy. Add the flour, mixing until smooth. Spread the batter in 7 cm (3 inch) circles, far apart, on greased and floured baking sheets.

Bake on the center oven rack for around 5 minutes.

Loosen the cookies with a sharp knife. Bend or roll immediately.

STAR SNAPS *approx. 60 cookies*

☆ This recipe won a prize in 1975.

- *Oven temp: 200°C (400°F), convection 175°C (350°F)*

175 g (¾ cup) stick margarine or butter, softened
1½ dl (⅔ cup) sugar
4 dl (1⅔ cups) all-purpose flour
1 teaspoon ground cardamom
Brushing and garnish:
1 egg, lightly beaten
25 g (¼ cup) sliced almonds
pearl sugar

▶ Beat the butter and sugar until fluffy. Add the remaining ingredients, mixing well. Wrap in plastic and refrigerate overnight.

Roll small balls (just under the size of a walnut) and place, far apart, on greased or parchment-lined baking sheets. Flatten to paper thin 9 cm (3 ¾ inches) rounds. Brush with beaten egg. Top with 4 almond slices in the center. Sprinkle with pearl sugar.

Bake on the center oven rack for around 8 minutes.

ALMOND LACE COOKIES *approx. 20 cookies*

- *Oven temp: 150°C (300°F), convection 150°C (300°F)*

50 g (½ cup) chopped almonds
50 g (⅓ cup) sliced almonds
1 dl (⅓ cup) sugar
100 g (7 tablespoons) stick margarine or butter

Star Snaps

Almond Lace Cookies

2 tablespoons all-purpose flour
2 tablespoons milk
I tablespoon light corn syrup or molasses

▶ Combine all the ingredients in a small saucepan. Heat, stirring constantly, until slightly thickened. Spoon mounds onto a well-greased or parchment-lined baking sheet.

Bake on the center oven rack for around 8 minutes, until golden.

Let cool slightly. Loosen with a sharp knife. Let cool completely on a flat surface.

OATMEAL LACE COOKIES

approx. 30 cookies

■ *Oven temp: 200 °C (400 °F), convection 175 °C (350 °F)*

75 g (5 tablespoons) stick margarine or
  butter
I dl (⅓ cup) rolled oats
I dl (½ cup) all-purpose flour
I dl (⅓ cup) sugar
2 tablespoons light cream or milk
2 tablespoons light corn syrup or molasses
¼ teaspoon baking powder

▶ Melt the butter in a small saucepan. Add the remaining ingredients. Heat, stirring constantly, until slightly thickened. Spoon mounds onto a greased or parchment-lined baking sheet.

Bake on the center oven rack for around 5 minutes.

Let cool slightly. Loosen with a sharp knife. Bend, if desired.

Oatmeal Lace Cookies

SÄTOFTA COOKIES

approx. 25 cookies

■ *Oven temp: 225 °C (425 °F), convection 200 °C (400 °F)*

4½ dl (2 cups) all-purpose flour
½ teaspoon baking powder
150 g (⅔ cup) stick margarine or butter
I dl (⅓ cup) whipping cream
2 teaspoons vanilla sugar or
  I teaspoon vanilla
50 g (⅓ cup)
  currants
sugar

▶ Combine the dry ingredients. Cut in the butter, add the cream and vanilla, mixing well. Knead in the currants.

Divide the dough in half. Form each half into 2½ cm (1 inch) thick ropes. Wrap in plastic and refrigerate for at least an hour.

Cut into 2 cm (¾ inch) pieces. Press into round cookies.

Pour sugar into a flat dish. Place one cookie at a time in the sugar and press until very thin and around 8 cm (3 inches) in diameter. Turn and press from the other side. Place on a greased or parchment-lined baking sheet.

Bake on the center oven rack for around 10 minutes.

SYRUP LACE COOKIES

approx. 50 cookies

- Oven temp: 200°C (400°F),
  convection 175°C (350°F)

150 g (scant ⅔ cup) stick margarine or butter
2 dl (¾ cup) sugar
½ dl (¼ cup) light or dark corn syrup
½ dl (3 tablespoons) whipping cream
2 dl (¾ cup) rolled oats
2 dl (1 cup) all-purpose flour
½ teaspoon baking powder
1 teaspoon vanilla sugar or ½ teaspoon
  vanilla extract

▶ Melt the butter in a saucepan. Add the remaining ingredients. Heat, stirring constantly, until slightly thickened. Spoon small mounds, far apart, onto greased or parchment-lined baking sheets. Bake on the center oven rack for around 5 minutes. Bend, if desired. Pictured on page 79.

DOUBLE SYRUP LACE
COOKIES *approx. 25 cookies*

The above cookies can be sandwiched together with chocolate cream (3 tablespoons butter, 1 tablespoon cocoa and 1 tablespoon powdered sugar) in between.

ALMOND-COCONUT LACE
COOKIES *approx. 50 cookies*

- Oven temp: 175°C (350°F),
  convection 175°C (350°F)

100 g (7 tablespoons) stick margarine or butter
2 dl (¾ cup) sugar
2 tablespoons light corn syrup or molasses
½ dl (3 tablespoons) whipping cream
2 dl (¾ cup) flaked coconut
2 dl (1 cup) slivered almonds
¾ dl (⅓ cup) all-purpose flour

▶ Melt the butter and let it cool. Add the remaining ingredients, stirring to combine. Spoon small mounds, far apart, onto greased or parchment-lined baking sheets.
Bake on the center oven rack for around 8 minutes. Let cool slightly before removing with a sharp knife. Let cool completely on a flat surface, or bend.

MILLET LACE COOKIES

approx. 30 cookies

These cookies are gluten-free.

- Oven temp: 175°C (350°F),
  convection 175°C (350°F)

75 g (5 tablespoons) stick margarine or butter
1 dl (½ cup) sugar
½ teaspoon vanilla sugar or ¼ teaspoon vanilla
2 tablespoons whipping cream
2 tablespoons light corn syrup or molasses
1 dl (⅓ cup) millet flakes
1 dl (½ cup) gluten-free fine flour mix
¼ teaspoon baking powder.

▶ Melt the butter and stir in the remaining ingredients. Spoon small mounds, far apart, on greased or parchment-lined baking sheets.
Bake on the center oven rack for around 8 minutes. Let cool slightly before removing with a sharp knife. Bend, if desired.

Coconut Almond Lace Cookies

Millet Lace Cookies

MARSTRAND COOKIES

approx. 75 cookies

- *Oven temp: 175°C (350°F), convection 175°C (350°F)*

100 g (7 tablespoons) stick margarine or butter

3½ dl (1½ cups) all-purpose flour

2½ dl (1 cup) potato starch or 3 dl (1¼ cups) cornstarch

1 teaspoon hornsalt or 2 teaspoons baking powder

¾ dl (⅓ cup) sugar

1½ dl (⅔) cup whipping cream

▶ Melt the butter and let it cool.

Combine the dry ingredients in a bowl. Add the cream and melted butter, mixing well. Cover and refrigerate for a couple of hours.

Roll the dough into a thin sheet. Prick with a fork. Cut 6 cm (2¼ inch) round cookies. Make a small hole at one side, if desired. Place on a greased or parchment-lined baking sheet.

Bake on the center oven rack for around 10 minutes. Pictured on page 105.

ANISE STARS *approx. 50 cookies*

- *Oven temp: 200°C (400°F), convection 200°C (400°F)*

2½ dl (1 cup) all-purpose flour

½ dl (3 tablespoons) sugar

1 teaspoon crushed anise seed

100 g (7 tablespoons) cold stick margarine or butter

1 egg yolk

Glaze:

1 dl (½ cup) powdered sugar

1–2 tablespoons water or anise liqueur

½ teaspoon crushed anise seed

red or green food coloring

pink sugar balls

▶ Place the dry ingredients in a food processor. Dice the butter and add with the egg yolk. Pulse until the dough begins to form a ball. Wrap in plastic and refrigerate or around an hour.

Roll the dough into a 3–4 mm (¼ inch) thick sheet. Cut out small stars with a cookie cutter. Place on a greased or parchment-lined baking sheet.

Bake on the center oven rack for 5–8 minutes. Let cool on a rack.

Mix powdered sugar, liquid and anise until smooth. Tint with food coloring. Spread the glaze over the cookies and garnish with pink sugar balls.

ARCHIPELAGO COOKIES *approx. 35 cookies*

- *Oven temp: 175°C (350°F), convection 175°C (350°F)*

150 g (⅔ cup) stick margarine or butter, softened

1 dl (½ cup) sugar

1 dl (½ cup) chopped walnuts

3 dl (1⅓ cups) all-purpose flour

½ teaspoon baking powder

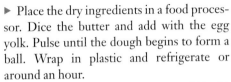

▶ Beat the butter and sugar until light and fluffy. Add the remaining ingredients, mixing well. Wrap in plastic and refrigerate for at least an hour.

Roll the dough into a thin sheet between two pieces of plastic wrap. Remove the top layer of plastic and roll with a striated rolling pin for a patterned surface. Cut 6 cm (2¼ inch) round cookies. Place on a greased or parchment-lined baking sheet.

Bake on the center oven rack for around 15 minutes.

BROWN SUGAR COOKIES

approx. 125 cookies

- *Oven temp: 175°C (350°F), convection 175°C (350°F)*
- 200 g (¾ cup) stick margarine or butter, softened
- 3 dl (1¼ cups) dark brown sugar
- 1 teaspoon ground cardamom
- 1 teaspoon cinnamon
- 2 eggs
- 2 teaspoons baking powder
- 6 dl (2½ cups) all-purpose flour

Brushing and garnish:
Water
1½ dl (⅔ cup) pearl sugar
¾ dl (⅓ cup) chopped almonds
or 3 cinnamon sticks, crushed

▶ Beat the butter and sugar until light and fluffy. Add the cardamom, cinnamon and eggs. Combine the baking powder with around ⅓ of the flour. Knead in the remaining flour, but reserve some for rolling out. Wrap in plastic and refrigerate for a couple of hours, preferably overnight.

Roll the dough into a thin sheet and cut cookies using your choice of shape.

Brush the cookies with water. Mix the pearl sugar and almonds or cinnamon and dip the cookies. Place on a greased or parchment-lined baking sheet.

Bake on the center oven rack for around 10 minutes.

FOLDED COOKIES *approx. 40 cookies*

- *Oven temp: 175°C (350°F), convection 175°C (350°F)*
- 200 g (¾ cup) cold stick margarine or butter
- 4 dl (1⅔ cups) all-purpose flour
- 1 dl (½ cup) potato starch or cornstarch
- 1 dl (½ cup) powdered sugar

Brushing and garnish:
1 egg, lightly beaten
2 tablespoons chopped almonds
2 tablespoons pearl sugar

▶ Dice the butter and cut it into the dry ingredients, kneading lightly. Wrap in plastic and refrigerate for at least an hour.

Roll the dough into a 2–3 mm (¼ inch) thick sheet. Cut 6 cm (2¼ inches) round cookies. Fold over almost in half.

Brush with beaten egg. Mix the almonds and sugar and dip the cookies. Place on a greased or parchment-lined baking sheet.

Bake on the center oven rack for around 10 minutes.

FRIDA'S JAM FOLDS

approx. 40 cookies

Prepare Folded Cookies, but place a dab of jelly in the center of the cookie before folding over.

Frida's Jam Folds

Folded Cookies

Crispy Half-Moons

APRICOT TRIANGLES

approx. 40 cookies

- Oven temp: 175°C (350°F),
  convection 175°C (350°F)

125 g (½ cup) cold stick
  margarine or butter
1 dl (⅓ cup) sugar
grated zest of ½ lemon
3 dl (1¼ cups) all-
  purpose flour
1 egg yolk

Filling:
apricot marmalade

Brushing:
1 egg, lightly beaten

▶ Dice the butter and cut it into the dry ingredients. Add the egg yolk, mixing well. Wrap in plastic and refrigerate for at least an hour.

Roll the dough into a 3 mm (¼ inch) thick sheet. Cut into 5 cm (2 inch) squares with a pastry wheel. Place a small spoonful of marmalade in the center and fold one half of the dough over the other on the diagonal.

Place on a greased or parchment-lined baking sheet. Brush with beaten egg.

Bake on the center oven rack for around 10 minutes.

CRISPY HALF-MOONS

approx. 15 cookies

There are no eggs in these cookies.

- Oven temp: 225°C (425°F),
  convection 200°C (400°F)

175 g (¾ cup) cold stick margarine or butter
4 dl (1⅔ cups) all-purpose flour
4 tablespoons (¼ cup) whipping cream
3–4 small apples or pears
sugar
cinnamon, nutmeg or ginger

Garnish:
sugar

▶ Dice the butter and cut it into the flour. Add the cream and toss quickly together. Wrap in plastic and refrigerate for at least an hour.

Roll the dough into a 4 mm (¼ inch) thick sheet. Cut 10 cm (4 inch) round cookies.

Coarsely grate the apples or pears. Arrange a mound of fruit on one side of each cookie. Sprinkle the apples with sugar and cinnamon or nutmeg, the pears with ginger. Fold the other half of the circle over the fruit and press to seal.

Place on a rinsed baking sheet. Let rest on the sheet for 10 minutes.

Bake on the center oven rack for around 15 minutes.

Remove from the oven and immediately dip the cookies in sugar.

GRANDMOTHER'S JAM
POCKETS *approx. 30 cookies*

- Oven temp: 175°C (350°F),
  convection 175°C (350°F)

4 dl (1⅔ cups) all-purpose flour
1 dl (½ cup) potato starch or cornstarch
1 dl (½ cup) powdered sugar
200 g (¾ cup) cold stick margarine or butter

Brushing and garnish:
1 egg, lightly beaten
chopped almonds
pearl sugar

Filling:
thick preserves or jelly

▶ Combine the dry ingredients in a bowl. Dice the butter and cut it into the flour mixture. Add the egg, kneading lightly. Wrap in plastic and refrigerate for at least an hour.

Roll the dough into a thin sheet. Cut half the dough into rounds. Cut the remaining half into wreaths the same diameter as the rounds. Brush the wreaths with beaten egg and dip in almonds and sugar. Place on top of the round cookies. Fill the centers with preserves.

Place on a greased or parchment-lined baking sheet.

Bake on the center oven rack for around 10 minutes.

Pictured on page 79.

IAN'S SUGAR WREATHS
approx. 30 cookies

- Oven temp: 175 °C (350 °F),
  convection 175 °C (350 °F)

2 dl (1 cup) all-purpose flour
½ dl (¼ cup) sugar
½ teaspoon vanilla sugar or ¼ teaspoon vanilla extract
100 g (½ cup) cold stick margarine or butter
½ egg
Garnish:
candied cherries
sugar

▶ Place the flour, sugar and vanilla in a food processor. Dice the butter and add, pulsing until combined. Add the egg and process until the dough begins to form a ball. Cover with plastic and refrigerate for at least an hour.

Roll the dough into balls the size of a hazelnut (around ½ inch). Arrange 8 balls into a ring directly on a greased or parchment-lined baking sheet. Repeat. Cut candied cherries into strips and place between the balls.

Bake on the center oven rack for around 10 minutes.

Dip in sugar while still warm.

NAPOLEON HATS *approx. 50 cookies*

- Oven temp: 175 °C (350 °F), 175 °C (350 °F)

150 g (⅔ cup) cold stick margarine or butter
4 ¾ dl (2 cups) all-purpose flour
1 dl (½ cup) sugar
1 egg
Almond paste:
100 g (1 cup) ground almonds
1 ½ dl (⅔ cup) sugar
1 egg white
2 drops green food coloring (optional)
Garnish:
2 tablespoons powdered sugar
water

▶ Dice the butter and cut it into the dry ingredients. Add the egg, kneading lightly. Wrap in plastic and refrigerate for at least an hour.

Beat the almonds and sugar with the egg white until smooth. Tint green, if desired.

Roll out the dough, preferably between two sheets of plastic wrap. Cut 6 cm (2 ¼ inches) round cookies. Place a small ball of almond paste in the center of each cookie. Fold the dough up from three sides and press against the filling to hold in place. Place on a greased or parchment-lined baking sheet.

Bake on the center oven rack for around 10 minutes.

Cool completely. Sift powdered sugar over the cookies or glaze with powdered sugar mixed with a few drops of water.

Ian's Sugar Wreaths

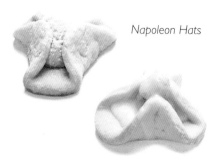

Napoleon Hats

PEPPERNUTS *approx. 30 cookies*

- Oven temp: 175°C (350°F),
  convection 175°C (350°F)

100 g (7 tablespoons) stick margarine or butter, softened
1 dl (⅓ cup) sugar
½ tablespoon light corn syrup or molasses
½ egg
1 teaspoon ground cardamom
1 teaspoon cinnamon
½ teaspoon ginger
around 3 ½ dl (1 ½ cups) all-purpose flour
1 teaspoon baking soda

Garnish:
15 blanched almonds, halved (optional)

▶ Beat the butter, sugar and molasses until light and fluffy. Add the egg, beating well. Stir in the dry ingredients, kneading until smooth.

Roll into balls and place on a greased or parchment-lined baking sheet. Push an almond half into each cookie, if desired.

Bake on the center oven rack for around 20 minutes.

Peppernuts should be completely dry and brown.

GRANDMOTHER'S LUNCH GINGERBREAD *approx. 100 cookies*

- Oven temp: 200°C (400°F),
  convection 175°C (350°F)

3 ½ dl (1 ½ cups) sugar
4 ½ dl (1 ¾ cups) light corn syrup
1 ½ teaspoons ground cloves
1 ½ teaspoon ginger
2 teaspoons cinnamon
150 g (⅔ cup) stick margarine or butter
3 eggs
1 dl (⅓–½ cup) milk
around 2 liters (8 ⅓ cups) all-purpose flour
2 teaspoons hornsalt (baking ammonia) or 4
  teaspoons baking powder
2 teaspoons baking powder

▶ Heat the sugar and syrup to boiling. Add the spices and butter. Whisk the eggs into the milk and then whisk into the sugar mixture. Let cool.

Combine the dry ingredients and add to the sugar mixture, mixing well. Transfer to a bowl. Sprinkle with a little flour and cover with plastic wrap. Let the dough rest at room temperature for 72 hours.

Form into large round balls. Place on a greased or parchment-lined baking sheet. Flatten slightly.

Bake on the center oven rack for 15 minutes.

FRENCH GINGERBREAD COOKIES *approx. 75 cookies*

- Oven temp: 175°C (350°F),
  convection 175°C (350°F)

200 g (¾ cup) stick margarine or butter
2 dl (¾ cup) sugar
1 dl (½ cup) light corn syrup or molasses
2 teaspoons ginger
2 teaspoons cinnamon
2 teaspoons ground cloves
1 teaspoon baking soda
around 6 dl (2½ cups) all-purpose flour
125 g (1 cup) chopped almonds

▶ Beat the butter, sugar and syrup until light and fluffy. Gradually add the dry ingredients and nuts, mixing well.

Turn the dough out onto a floured surface. Knead until smooth. Divide in half and form into thick logs. Flatten into a rectangular shape, if desired.

Wrap each log in plastic. Refrigerate for several hours or overnight.

Cut into thin slices with a sharp knife. Place on greased baking sheets.

Bake on the center oven rack for around 12 minutes.

GINGERBREAD COOKIES

approx. 175 cookies

- Oven temp: 175°C (350°F),
  convection 175°C (350°F)

1½ dl (⅔ cup) whipping cream
2½ dl (1 cup) sugar
1½ dl (⅔ cup) light corn syrup or molasses
1½ tablespoons ginger
½ teaspoon lemon extract or 1 teaspoon grated lemon zest
1 tablespoon baking soda stirred into 2 teaspoons water
8½ dl (3½ cups) all-purpose flour

▶ Lightly whip the cream. Add the sugar, syrup, ginger, lemon and soda. Beat for 3 minutes. Add most of the flour, kneading lightly. Cover and let rest at room temperature overnight.

Turn out onto a floured surface. Knead until smooth. Roll the dough into a thin sheet on a floured surface. Cut out different shapes with cookie cutters. Place them on cold greased or parchment-lined baking sheets.

Bake on the center oven rack for around 7 minutes.

Let cool on the baking sheets.

SKANSEN'S CHRISTMAS GINGERBREAD COOKIES *approx. 160 cookies*

- Oven temp: 200°C (400°F),
  convection 175°C (350°F)

1½ dl (⅔ cup) light or dark corn syrup
3 dl (1¼ cups) dark brown sugar
200 g (¾ cup) stick margarine or butter
1 large egg
2 teaspoons ground cloves
1 teaspoon ground bitter orange peel
1½ teaspoons baking soda
8 dl (3⅓ cups) all-purpose flour

▶ Heat the syrup to boiling and pour over the sugar and butter. Stir until cold. Add the eggs and spices. Stir the soda into 1 teaspoon cold water and add. Stir in most of the flour. Knead the dough well. Cover and let rest at room temperature overnight.

Roll the dough into a thin sheet on a floured board. Cut out different shapes with cookie cutters. Place them on greased or parchment-lined baking sheets.

Bake on the center oven rack for around 8 minutes.

Pictured at right: Gingerbread Cookies, top, and French Gingerbread Slices, bottom.

SPICY GINGERBREAD COOKIES

approx. 100 cookies

■ *Oven temp: 200°C (400°F),*
convection 175°C (350°F)

100 g (7 tablespoons) stick margarine or
    butter, softened
2½ dl (1 cup) dark brown sugar
1 dl (½ cup) light/dark corn/sugar syrup
1 dl (½ cup) whipping cream
2 teaspoons ginger
2 teaspoons cinnamon
2 teaspoons ground cloves
around 8½ dl (3½ cups) all-purpose flour
2 teaspoons baking soda

▶ Beat the butter, sugar and syrup until light
and fluffy. Add the cream and spices. Combine the flour and soda and add, kneading
until smooth. Cover and let rest at room
temperature overnight.

Roll the dough into a not-too-thin sheet.
Cut into shapes and place on cold greased or
parchment-lined baking sheets. Bake on the
center oven rack for around 8 minutes.

WHITE GINGERBREAD COOKIES

approx. 100 cookies

■ *Oven temp: 175°C (350°F),*
convection 175°C (350°F)

3½ dl (1½ cups) water
3½ dl (1½ cups) light corn syrup
4½ dl (1¾ cups) sugar
60 g (¼ cup) stick margarine or butter
2¾ teaspoons hornsalt (baking ammonia) or
    5 teaspoons baking powder
2½ liters (10⅓ cups)
    all-purpose flour
Garnish:
3 dl (1¼ cups) powdered sugar
½ egg white
food coloring

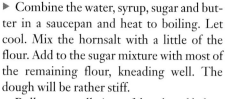

▶ Combine the water, syrup, sugar and butter in a saucepan and heat to boiling. Let
cool. Mix the hornsalt with a little of the
flour. Add to the sugar mixture with most of
the remaining flour, kneading well. The
dough will be rather stiff.

Roll out a small piece of dough and bake a
trial cookie. Add more flour if necessary.

Cut out different shapes with cookie cutters. Place them on greased or parchment-
lined baking sheets.

Bake them on the center oven rack for
around 7 minutes, until light golden.

Garnish with powdered sugar mixed with
egg white. Tint with a few drops of food coloring, if desired.

GLUTEN-FREE GINGERBREAD
COOKIES *approx. 60 cookies*

■ *Oven temp: 200°C (400°F),*
convection 175°C (350°F)

50 g (3 tablespoons) stick margarine or butter
1 teaspoon cinnamon
1 teaspoon ginger
1 teaspoon ground cloves
½ dl (3 tablespoons) light or dark corn syrup
½ dl (¼ cup) sugar
1 egg
¾ teaspoon baking soda
3½ dl (1½ cups) gluten-free flour mix

▶ Place the butter and spices in a bowl. Heat
the syrup and sugar to boiling. Pour over the
butter and stir until cold. Stir in the egg.

Combine the dry ingredients and knead
into the butter mixture. Cover and refrigerate overnight.

Turn the dough out onto a surface sprinkled with gluten-free mix. Knead until
smooth, using more mix, if necessary.

Roll the dough into a not-too-thin sheet on
a flour or plastic covered board. Cut out different shapes with cookie cutters. Place them
on greased or parchment-lined baking sheets.

Bake on the center oven rack for around 5
minutes.

Birgits Favorites, page 145, top; two Individual Princess Cakes, page 159; and Christmas Stars, bottom.

Pastries ▶

Decorating with chocolate

To melt chocolate. Use the correct temperature for a shiny surface. For the best results, read the directions on the package.

In the microwave oven. Place the chocolate in a bowl (not metal) and melt it on "high", maximum 800W, for 30 seconds to two minutes, depending upon the quantity. The bowl should be left uncovered. Stir occasionally.

On a hot cake. Bake the cake until done. Remove it from the oven. Grate or shave the chocolate directly onto the hot cake and spread with a spatula. See picture 1.

In a water bath. Break the chocolate into pieces and place them in a small bowl.

Add coconut fat or oil, if desired. Place over a saucepan of warm water, 60–70°C (140–160°F). Do not allow the water to get too hot.

The sides of the bowl should fit tightly against the saucepan. Do not allow water or steam to get into the chocolate. See picture 2.

To decorate.
Dipping. Dip the cake or cookie into the melted chocolate. Twist and let any excess chocolate drip off.

Piping with a bag. Break the chocolate into pieces and place them in a small plastic bag. Seal. Place in hot water and let the chocolate melt. Cut a tiny hole in one corner of the bag. Pipe as desired.

Decorative sheets. Spread the melted chocolate on baking parchment. Let cool on a flat surface. Cut into diagonal rectangles or squares.

Shreds and rolls. Make a small, thick sheet of melted chocolate on baking parchment. Let it cool, but do not allow it to stiffen completely. Using a cheese plane, make thin wide pieces, then roll together. They almost roll by themselves.

CHOCO-COCO SQUARES

30–35 squares

A popular cake with many names, such as mocha squares, everyday squares and big batch squares.

■ *Oven temp: 175 °C (350 °F),*
  convection 175 °C (350 °F)

150 g (⅔ cup) stick margarine or butter
2 eggs
3 dl (1 ¼ cups) sugar
2 teaspoons vanilla sugar or 1 teaspoon
  vanilla extract
1 tablespoon sifted cocoa
4 ½ dl (2 cups) all-purpose flour
2 teaspoons baking powder
1 ½ dl (⅔ cup) milk

Frosting:
75 g (5 tablespoons) stick margarine or butter
1–2 tablespoons cold coffee
1 tablespoon sifted cocoa
2 teaspoons vanilla sugar or 1 teaspoon
  vanilla extract
3 ½ dl (1 ½ cups) powdered sugar

Garnish: flaked coconut

▶ Grease and flour a 30 × 40 cm (12 × 16 inch) sheet cake pan.

Melt the butter and let it cool. Beat the eggs and sugar until light yellow and very thick. Add the dry ingredients alternately with the milk and melted butter. Pour into the prepared pan.

Bake on a low oven rack for around 15 minutes.

Let cool. For the frosting, melt the butter and stir in the remaining ingredients. Spread over the cake. Sprinkle with coconut. Cut into squares.

JAM SQUARES *18 squares*

■ *Oven temp: 200 °C (400 °F),*
  convection 175 °C (350 °F)

4 ½ dl (2 cups) flour
1 dl (½ cup) sugar
1 tablespoon baking powder
150 g (⅔ cup) cold stick margarine or butter
1 egg
2 dl (¾ cup) lingonberry (or raspberry)
  preserves

Streusel topping:
1 ½ dl (⅔ cup) rolled oats
1 dl (⅓ cup) sugar
1 teaspoon vanilla sugar or ½ teaspoon vanilla extract
50 g (3 tablespoons) stick margarine or
  butter

▶ Grease a 20 × 30 cm (8 × 12 inch or 10 inch square) pan.

Combine the dry ingredients. Dice the butter and cut it into the flour mixture. Add the egg, mixing well.

Press the dough into the prepared pan. Spread the preserves over the dough.

Combine the oats, sugar and vanilla. Melt the butter and pour over the oat mixture, stirring well. Spread over the preserves.

Bake on a low oven rack for around 20 minutes.

Let cool. Cut into squares.

MANOR BARS *25 squares*

☆ This recipe won a prize in 1965.

- *Oven temp: 175°C (350°F), convection 175°C (350°F)*

100 g (7 tablespoons) stick margarine or butter, softened
1 ½ dl (⅔ cup) powdered sugar
2 egg yolks
1 egg
grated zest of ½ lemon
2 dl (1 cup) all-purpose flour
½ teaspoon baking powder

Garnish:
2 egg whites
4 tablespoons (¼ cup) sugar
25 g (⅓ cup) sliced almonds
1 dl (⅓ cup) raisins or currants

▶ Grease and flour or line a 20 × 30 cm (8 × 12 inch or 10 inch square) pan with baking parchment.

Beat the butter and sugar until light and fluffy. Add the remaining ingredients, mixing well. Spread into the prepared pan.

Beat the egg whites until stiff. Add the sugar and beat for a few minutes more, until thick and glossy. Spread over the cake mixture. Sprinkle with nuts and raisins.

Bake on a low oven rack for 15–20 minutes, until golden on top and dry inside.

Cool completely before cutting into squares.

DELICATE GINGERBREAD
18 squares

- *Oven temp: 175°C (350°F), convection 175°C (350°F)*

50 g (3 tablespoons) stick margarine or butter
2 eggs
3 dl (1 ¼ cups) sugar
3 dl (1 ¼ cups) all-purpose flour
½ teaspoon baking soda
1 ½ teaspoons cinnamon
½ teaspoon ginger
1 ½ dl (⅔ cup) dairy sour cream

Frosting:
75 g (5 tablespoons) stick margarine or butter
grated zest of 1 orange
1 tablespoon orange juice
3 ½ dl (1 ½ cups) sifted powdered sugar
thin orange slices

▶ Grease and flour a 30 × 40 cm (12 × 16 inch) sheet cake pan.

Melt the butter and let it cool.

Beat the eggs and sugar until light yellow and very thick. Combine the dry ingredients and add. Stir in the sour cream and the butter, mixing well.

Pour into the prepared pan.

Bake on a low oven rack for 25–30 minutes.

Let cool for 5 minutes, then remove from the pan. Let cool completely.

For the frosting, beat all the ingredients until smooth and shiny. Spread over the cake. Cut into squares and garnish each with thin orange slices that have been twisted to form an S.

NUNS *approx. 30 cakes*

- *Oven temp: 175 °C (350 °F), convection 175 °C (350 °F)*

150 g (⅔ cup) stick margarine or butter
125 g (1 cup) ground almonds
2 dl (¾ cup) powdered sugar
1 tablespoon vanilla sugar or ½ teaspoon vanilla extract
3 egg whites
1 dl (½ cup) all-purpose flour
2 egg whites

Glaze:
2 dl (¾ cup) sifted powdered sugar
1 tablespoon instant coffee granules
1 ½ tablespoons water

▶ Grease and flour 30 individual tins or wide muffin pans.

Brown the butter until light golden. Let cool.

Combine the almonds, sugar, vanilla and 3 egg whites. Beat at high speed for 3 minutes. Add the butter and flour, stirring to combine. Beat the 2 remaining egg whites until stiff and fold into the almond mixture.

Spoon into the prepared tins.

Bake on the center oven rack for 12–15 minutes.

Let cool for a few minutes, then carefully remove from the tins.

For the glaze, combine all ingredients and beat until smooth and shiny. Spread over the cakes.

KERSTIN'S ALMOND SQUARES
24 squares

- *Oven temp: 175 °C (350 °F), convection 175 °C (350 °F)*

400 g (14 ounces) almond paste
grated zest of ½ orange
juice of 1 orange
4 eggs

Garnish:
125 g (4 ounces) semi-sweet chocolate
sliced almonds (optional)

▶ Grease and flour or line a 20 × 30 cm (8 × 12 inch or 10 inch square) tin with baking parchment.

Coarsely grate the almond paste. Add the orange juice and zest. Separate the eggs, placing the whites in a large mixer bowl. Beat the egg yolks, one at a time, into the almond mixture, beating well after each.

Beat the egg whites until stiff. Carefully fold into the almond mixture. Spread into the prepared pan.

Bake on a low oven rack for 25–30 minutes.

Grate the chocolate over the warm cake. Spread to cover the entire cake. Sprinkle with almonds, if desired. Cut into squares.

BROWNIES _24 squares_

These should be slightly chewy. To retain moisture, store with a piece of white bread.

- ■ _Oven temp: 150°C (300°F), convection 150°C (300°F)_
150 g (⅔ cup) butter
¾ dl (⅓ cup) cocoa
3 eggs
3 dl (1¼ cups) sugar
2½ dl (1 cup) all-purpose flour
½ teaspoon baking powder
100 g (¾ cup) chopped walnuts

▶ Grease and flour or line a 20 × 35 cm (9 × 13 inch) pan with baking parchment.

Melt the butter and add the cocoa, stirring until smooth. Let cool.

Beat the eggs and sugar until light yellow and very thick. Stir in the chocolate mixture with the dry ingredients. Spread in the prepared pan.

Bake on a low oven rack for 25–30 minutes.

Let cool slightly. Cut into squares with a sharp knife.

FROSTED BROWNIES

Prepare the above recipe. Frost the bars with melted chocolate and garnish with walnut halves.

TUILES _around 25_

There are many old recipes for these cookies. The amount of butter and flour can vary.

- ■ _Oven temp: 200°C (400°F), convection 175°C (350°F)_
150 g (⅔ cup) stick margarine or butter
1 dl (½ cup) sugar
2 eggs
1½ dl (⅔ cup) all-purpose flour

Garnish:
pearl sugar
¾ dl (⅓ cup) chopped almonds

▶ Melt the butter and let it cool. Stir in the sugar. Add the eggs, one at a time, beating well after each. Stir in the flour.

Grease and heat a Swedish pancake pan or a non-stick pan. Place ½ tablespoon batter in each indentation of the pancake pan or 4–5 mounds in the non-stick pan.

Bake on the center oven rack for a couple of minutes. Remove from the oven and sprinkle with pearl sugar and almonds. Return to the oven and bake for 6 more minutes, until golden.

Bend over a rolling pin.

Brownies

Frosted Brownies

Mint Squares

MINT SQUARES *20 squares*

- ■ *Oven temp: 175°C (350°F),*
  convection 175°C (350°F)

Sponge base:
3 eggs
1½ dl (⅔ cup) sugar
¾ dl (⅓ cup) all-purpose flour
¾ dl (⅓ cup) potato starch or cornstarch
1 teaspoon baking powder

Filling:
3 gelatin sheets
2 dl (¾ cup) whipping cream
1 egg
3 tablespoons sugar
15 drops peppermint extract

Frosting:
4 dl (1⅔ cups) powdered sugar
1 egg white
2 tablespoons lemon juice
25 g (2 tablespoons) hydrogenated coconut fat
8 drops peppermint extract
1–2 drops green food coloring
pistachio nuts

▶ Grease and flour a 20 × 30 cm (8 × 12 inch or 10 inch square) pan.

Beat the eggs and sugar until light yellow and very thick. Combine the dry ingredients and fold into the egg mixture. Pour into the prepared pan.

Bake on a low oven rack for around 20 minutes. Let cool for 5 minutes, then remove from the pan. Let cool completely on a rack. Cut into 5 × 5 cm (2 inch) squares.

Soak the gelatin in cold water for at least 5 minutes to soften. Squeeze excess water from the gelatin and melt in a saucepan or microwave oven. Whisk into the egg mixture. Whip the cream and fold into the egg mixture. Stir in the mint extract.

Halve the cake squares horizontally. Spread the filling between the halves. Refrigerate until set.

Beat the powdered sugar, egg white and lemon juice until smooth. Melt the coconut oil and add. Stir in the mint extract and tint it light green.

Glaze the cakes. Garnish each with a pistachio nut. Refrigerate until set.

HALF-MOONS *20 cakes*

- ■ *Oven temp: 200°C (400°F),*
  convection 175°C (350°F)

1 batch Tuile batter

Filling:
1 dl (½ cup) applesauce

Glaze:
2 dl (¾ cup) sifted powdered sugar
1½–2 tablespoons water
green food coloring
chopped pistachios or almonds

▶ Prepare the Tuile batter. Grease a Swedish pancake pan and spoon 2 teaspoons batter into each indentation.

Bake on the center oven rack for around 8 minutes.

Transfer the cookies to a rack to cool.

Spread applesauce on half the cookies. Top with the remaining cookies. Halve to make half-moons.

Beat the powdered sugar and water into a thick glaze. Tint it green. Glaze the cookies and sprinkle with chopped nuts.

Half-Moons

MILAN LOGS *30 cookies*

- *Oven temp: 200°C (400°F),*
  convection 175°C (350°F)

4½ dl (2 cups) all-purpose flour
¾ dl (⅓ cup) sugar
200 g (¾ cup) stick margarine or butter
1 egg yolk

Filling:
200 g (7 ounces) almond paste
3 egg whites

Brushing and garnish:
egg white
sugar
50 g (½ cup) sliced almonds

▶ Combine the dry ingredients. Dice the butter and cut into the flour mixture. Add the egg yolk, mixing lightly. Wrap in plastic and refrigerate for at least three hours.

Grate the almond paste. Add the egg whites, beating until smooth.

Roll the dough into a sheet on a floured surface. Cut into 8 × 6 cm (3 ½ × 2 ¼ inch) rectangles. Spoon a thin strip of almond paste mixture along one long end. Roll up into 2–3 cm (1 inch) thick logs. Place on a greased or parchment-lined baking sheet. Brush with egg white. Sprinkle with a little sugar and almonds.

Bake on the center oven rack for around 10 minutes, until golden.

MIGNON COOKIES *34 cookies*

☆ This recipe won a prize in 1945.

- *Oven temp: 175°C (350°F),*
  convection 175°C (350°F)

175 g (¾ cup) stick margarine or butter, softened
2 dl (¾ cup) sugar
1 egg
100 g (¾ cup) ground almonds
6 dl (2 ½ cups) all-purpose flour

Filling:
3 egg yolks
2 tablespoons all-purpose flour
3 dl (1 ¼ cups) whipping cream
2 teaspoons vanilla sugar or 1 teaspoon vanilla extract

Garnish:
1 ½ dl (⅔ cup) sifted powdered sugar
1 tablespoon water
red jelly

Mignon Cookies

Milan Logs

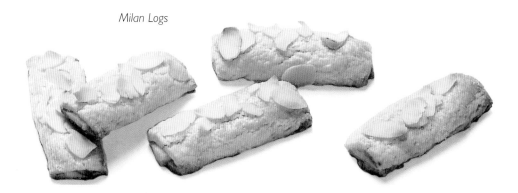

▶ Beat the butter and sugar until light and fluffy. Add the egg and almonds. Add the flour, kneading lightly. Wrap in plastic and refrigerate for at least two hours.

Combine the egg yolks, flour and cream in a saucepan. Simmer, stirring constantly, until thickened. Remove from the heat. Stir in the vanilla. Let cool.

Roll the dough into a thin sheet. Cut 5–6 cm (2–2 ½ inch) round cookies. Place on a greased or parchment-lined baking sheet.

Bake on the center oven rack for 7–10 minutes.

Let cool.

Sandwich the cookies with the vanilla cream in between.

Combine the powdered sugar and water, beating until smooth. Spread over the cookies. Garnish with jelly.

SCANIA HILLS *around 45*

■ *Oven temp. 200 °C (400 °F),*
convection 175 °C (350 °F)

Butter cookie base:
4 dl (1 ⅔ cups) all-purpose flour
½ dl (3 tablespoons) sugar
175 g (¾ cup) cold stick margarine or butter
1 egg yolk

Almond filling:
125 g (1 cup) ground almonds
1 ½ dl (⅔ cup) sugar
1 egg yolk

or

250 g (9 ounces) almond paste

Tosca mixture:
1 ½ dl (⅔ cup) chopped nuts
¾ dl (⅓ cup) sugar
75 g (5 tablespoons) stick margarine or butter
1 ½ tablespoons all-purpose flour
1 tablespoon milk

▶ Combine the dry ingredients. Dice the butter and cut it into the flour mixture until crumbly. Add the egg yolk, mixing well. Wrap in plastic and refrigerate for at least an hour.

Combine the almonds and sugar. Beat in the egg white. Or use prepared almond paste.

Divide the cookie base into 4 pieces. Roll each into a 10 × 30 cm (4 × 12 inch) sheet. Spoon a thin strip of almond filling down the center and fold over the edges. Place the lengths, seam side down, on a greased or parchment-lined baking sheet.

Partially bake on the center oven rack for 8 minutes.

Meanwhile, prepare the Tosca mixture. Combine all the ingredients in a saucepan. Heat carefully, stirring constantly, until slightly thickened.

Remove the cakes from the oven. Spread with the Tosca mixture. Bake for 7–8 minutes more, until golden.

Let cool, then cut into 2 cm (1 inch) wide diagonal pieces.

Vanilla Hearts

VANILLA HEARTS *16 pastries*

- Oven temp: 200°C (400°F),
  convection 175°C (350°F)

4 dl (1 ⅔ cups) all-purpose flour
1 dl (½ cup) potato starch or cornstarch
¾–1 dl (⅓–½ cup) sugar
200 g (¾ cup) cold stick margarine or butter

Vanilla cream filling:
1 ½ dl (⅔ cup) light cream
1 egg yolk
2 teaspoons sugar
1 tablespoon potato starch or cornstarch
2 teaspoons vanilla sugar or 1 teaspoon
  vanilla extract

Garnish:
powdered sugar

▶ Grease 16 individual heart tins.

Combine the dry ingredients. Dice the butter and cut it into the flour mixture, tossing quickly together. Cover with plastic and refrigerate for at least two hours.

Combine all the ingredients except vanilla in a saucepan. Simmer, stirring constantly, until thickened. Let cool, then stir in the vanilla.

Roll the dough into a rather thick sheet. Press into the heart tins. Fill with vanilla cream and cover with another layer of dough. Place the tins on a baking sheet.

Bake on a low oven rack for around 15 minutes.

Carefully remove from the tins. When completely cool, sift powdered sugar over.

LITTLE LEMON TARTS
around 12 pastries

These are similar to Vanilla Hearts, but they are filled with lemon cream.

- Oven temp: 200°C (400°F),
  convection 175°C (350°F)

1 batch Vanilla Heart dough

Lemon cream filling:
2 eggs
1 ½ dl (⅔ cup) sugar
grated zest and juice of 1 lemon
100 g (7 tablespoons) stick margarine or butter

Garnish:
powdered sugar

▶ Grease oval or round tartlet tins.

Prepare the Vanilla Heart dough. Cover with plastic and refrigerate for at least two hours.

Beat the eggs and sugar until light yellow and very thick. Add the lemon zest and juice. Melt the butter in a saucepan. Whisk in the egg mixture. Heat, whisking constantly, until thickened.

Roll out the dough or press it into the tins. Fill with lemon cream and cover with another layer of dough. Place the tins on a baking sheet.

Bake on a low oven rack for around 15 minutes.

Carefully remove from the tins. When completely cool, sift powdered sugar over.

Vanilla Hearts

Little Lemon Tarts

MAZARINS *18 pastries*

☆ This recipe won a prize in 1965. There are two suggested fillings – the one using almond paste is quicker to prepare.

- *Oven temp: 200°C (400°F), convection 175°C (350°F)*

3 dl (1 ¼ cups) all-purpose flour
½ teaspoon baking powder
3 tablespoons sugar
100 g (7 tablespoons) cold stick margarine or butter
½ egg

Filling 1:
75 g (5 tablespoons) stick margarine or butter
3 eggs
1 ½ dl (⅔ cup) sugar
150 g (1 ⅓ cups) ground almonds

Filling 2:
50 g (3 tablespoons) stick margarine or butter, softened
150 g (5 ounces) almond paste
2 eggs
3 tablespoons all-purpose flour
½ teaspoon baking powder

Garnish:
2 dl (¾ cup) sifted powdered sugar + water
or
½ dl (3 tablespoons) powdered sugar

▶ Grease individual oval tins.
Combine the dry ingredients. Dice the butter and cut it into the flour mixture. Add the egg, mixing well. Wrap in plastic and refrigerate for several hours.

Press or roll out the dough and line the tins.

Filling 1: Melt the butter and let it cool. Beat the eggs and sugar until light yellow and very thick. Stir in the almonds and melted butter.

Filling 2: Beat the butter until fluffy. Grate the almond paste and add. Beat in the eggs, one at a time, beating well after each. Stir in the flour and baking powder.

Spoon one of the fillings into the pastry shells.

Bake in the bottom half of the oven for around 15 minutes.

Let cool for a few minutes, then remove from the pans.

Beat the sugar and water until smooth. Spread over the tops or sift over powdered sugar.

MAZARIN TART

You can also bake a tart from this recipe. Use a 25 cm (10 inch) springform pan. Bake the tart at 175°C (350°F) for around 20 minutes. Pictured on page 163.

POLYNESIANS *18 pastries*

These pastries are also called Emperor's Crowns.

- ■ *Oven temp: 175°C (350°F),*
  convection 175°C (350°F)

2½ dl (1 cup) all-purpose flour
½ dl (3 tablespoons) sugar
100 g (7 tablespoons) cold stick margarine or butter
1 small egg or 1 egg yolk

Filling:
100 g (1 cup) ground hazelnuts or almonds
3 dl (1¼ cups) sifted powdered sugar
2–3 egg whites

▶ Grease 18 individual tartlet tins.

Combine the dry ingredients. Dice the butter and cut it into the flour mixture. Add the egg, mixing well. Wrap in plastic and refrigerate for at least an hour.

Roll out part of the dough and cut ½ cm (¼ inch) strips. Press the remaining dough into the tins. It should not be too thin at the top.

Combine the nuts and sugar. Add the egg whites and mix until smooth. Spoon into the pastry shells. Do not fill more than ⅔ full. Place the strips in an X over the filling.

Place on a baking sheet. Bake on a low oven rack for 10–15 minutes, until golden.

Remove from the tins while still warm.

HELENA TARTS *20 pastries*

These pastries are similar to Polynesians but with a short crust pastry shell.

- ■ *Oven temp: 175°C (350°F),*
  convection 175°C (350°F)

4 dl (1⅔ cups) all-purpose flour
125 g (½ cup) cold stick margarine or butter
2 tablespoons water

Filling:
100 g (1 cup) ground almonds
3 dl (1¼ cups) sifted powdered sugar
3 small egg whites

▶ Place the flour in a mound on the work surface. Dice the butter and cut it into the flour. Add the water and mix quickly together. Wrap in plastic and refrigerate for several hours.

Combine the almonds, sugar and egg whites, mixing until smooth.

Roll the dough into a thin sheet. Cut out rounds and place in greased small tartlet pans. Cut the remaining dough into narrow strips.

Fill the pastry shells with the almond mixture. Place the strips in an X over the filling.

Place on a baking sheet. Bake on a low oven rack for around 15 minutes, until golden.

TRUFFLE TARTS *15 pastries*

- *Oven temp: 200 °C (400 °F),*
  convection 175 °C (350 °F)

3 dl (1 ¼ cups) all-purpose flour
¾ dl (⅓ cup) cornstarch
¾ dl (⅓ cup) sifted powdered sugar
1 teaspoon vanilla sugar or ½ teaspoon
  vanilla extract
150 g (⅔ cup) cold butter
1 ½ tablespoon light corn syrup

Chocolate truffle filling:
1 dl (½ cup) whipping cream
½ dl (¼ cup) milk
150 g (5 ounces) semi-sweet chocolate
1 egg yolk

Garnish:
powdered sugar

▶ Grease individual tartlet tins.

Combine the dry ingredients on the work surface. Dice the butter and cut it into the flour mixture. Add the syrup, kneading quickly. Roll out ⅓ of the dough and cut out small round cookies. Place on a greased baking sheet.

Bake on the center oven rack for around 4 minutes.

Press the remaining dough into the tins and press up the sides. The edge should be an even thickness.

Bake on a low oven rack for 8–10 minutes.

Immediately remove from the tins and let cool.

Heat the cream and milk to boiling. Chop the chocolate and add, stirring until melted. Refrigerate until cold.

Beat until fluffy. Add the egg yolk. Fill the pastry shells with the truffle mixture.

Top with the little round cookies. Sift powdered sugar over.

Store in the refrigerator.

ITALIAN CHOCOLATE PASTRIES 6 pastries

- Oven temp: 250°C (450°F), convection 225°C (425°F)

Sponge bases:
3 eggs
1 ½ dl (⅔ cup) sugar
2 tablespoons potato starch or cornstarch
2 tablespoons all purpose flour
1 tablespoon cocoa
1 tablespoon crushed instant coffee granules
1 teaspoon baking powder

Filling:
100 g (7 tablespoons) stick margarine or butter, softened
1 ½ dl (⅔ cup) sifted powdered sugar
2 tablespoons cocoa
1 ½ teaspoons crushed instant coffee granules
½ teaspoon vanilla
1 egg yolk
1–2 tablespoons coffee liqueur (optional)

Garnish:
100 g (3 ounces) semi-sweet chocolate
1 tablespoon oil
1 ½ dl (⅔ cup) sifted powdered sugar
1 tablespoon water
2 drops peppermint oil

▶ Line a 30 × 40 cm (12 × 16 inch) sheet cake pan with baking parchment.

Beat the eggs and sugar until light yellow and very thick. Combine the remaining ingredients and sift into the egg mixture. Fold until evenly combined.

Pour into the prepared pan. Bake on the center oven rack for around 5 minutes. Turn out onto sugared paper and let cool.

For the filling, beat the butter, sugar, cocoa, coffee and vanilla until smooth. Beat in the egg yolk and the coffee liqueur, if desired. Beat until smooth.

Spread half the chocolate cream over the cake. Measure and cut out 5 cm (2 inch) wide strips, around 36 cm (14 inches) long. Roll tightly together and stand up on the cut side.

Melt the chocolate and oil in a water bath or in the microwave oven. Beat until smooth and shiny.

Dip or brush the cakes with chocolate. Place on a rack to set.

Spoon the remaining chocolate into a pastry bag with a small plain tip and make tiny mounds around the outer edge.

Beat the sugar, water and peppermint oil until smooth. Spoon into a pastry bag with a plain tip and pipe a white "lid" within the chocolate. Let set.

PARISIAN WAFFLES 10 pastries

☆ This recipe won a prize in 1945. They are also called French Waffles.

- Oven temp: 225°C (425°F), convection 200°F (400°C)

100 g (7 tablespoons) cold stick margarine or butter
2 ½ dl (1 cup) all-purpose flour
1–2 tablespoons water

For rolling:
sugar

Filling:
100 g (7 tablespoons) soft butter
1 ½ dl (⅔ cup) sifted powdered sugar
1 egg yolk
2 teaspoons vanilla sugar or 1 teaspoon vanilla extract

▶ Grease 2 baking sheets.

Dice the butter and cut into the flour. Add the water, kneading quickly. Wrap in plastic and refrigerate for several hours.

Roll out the dough to just under ½ cm (¼ inch) thick. Cut 6 cm (2 ¼ inch) round cookies. Place on sugared baking parchment and roll into ovals with a patterned rolling pin. Transfer to the baking sheets.

Bake on the center oven rack for 6–8 minutes, or until they are golden and crispy.

For the filling, beat the butter and sugar until light and fluffy. Add the egg and vanilla, beating until smooth. Sandwich two cookies with filling in between.

Pictured at right: Italian Chocolate Pastries, top; Parisian Waffles, center; and Alliance Twists, page 136, bottom.

FINNISH BUTTER BOATS

approx. 30 pastries

- Oven temp: 200 °C (400 °F),
  convection 175 °C (350 °F)
3 dl (1 ¼ cups) all-purpose flour
½ dl (3 tablespoons) sugar
125 g (½ cup) cold stick margarine or butter
1 small egg yolk

Filling:
75 g (5 tablespoons) soft butter
1 dl (⅓ cup) sifted powdered sugar
½ teaspoon vanilla sugar or ¼ teaspoon
  vanilla extract
1 egg white, lightly beaten

Glaze:
2 dl (¾ cup) sifted powdered sugar
1 ½–2 tablespoons water
green or red food coloring

▶ Grease small oval boat tins.

In a food processor, pulse all ingredients together until the dough starts to form a ball. Wrap in plastic and refrigerate for around 30 minutes.

Press the dough into the tins and place on a baking sheet. Bake on the center oven rack for around 10 minutes.

Let cool slightly, then remove from the tins.

Combine all ingredients for the filling, beating until smooth. Spoon into the cold pastry boats. Stir the sugar and water together until smooth. Tint light green or pink. Spread over the buttercream.

ALLIANCE TWISTS *approx. 35 pastries*

These lovely pastries are made with both butter cookie dough and puff pastry.

- Oven temp: 225 °C (425 °F), convection
  200 °C (400 °F)

Butter cookie dough:
2 ½ dl (1 cup) all-purpose flour
½ dl (3 tablespoons) sugar
100 g (7 tablespoons) cold stick margarine
  or butter
½ egg
½ teaspoon baking powder

Puff pastry:
150 g (⅔ cup) cold stick margarine or butter
2 ½ dl (1 cup) all-purpose flour
1 ½ tablespoons cream
1 ½ tablespoons water

Brushing and garnish:
1 egg, lightly beaten
chopped almonds
pearl sugar

▶ Grease or line a baking sheet with parchment paper.

In a food processor, pulse all ingredients together until the dough starts to form a ball. Wrap in plastic and refrigerate for around 30 minutes.

Dice the butter and cut it into the flour. Add the remaining ingredients, kneading quickly until smooth. Wrap in plastic and refrigerate for around an hour.

Roll out and fold into thirds. Repeat the rolling and folding 3 more times. Wrap in plastic and refrigerate for a while between each folding.

Roll out each dough separately into rectangular sheets around 20 cm (8 inches) wide and 2–3 mm (¼ inch) thick. Place them on top of each other and press down lightly with a rolling pin. Trim the edges.

Cut the dough crosswise into 1 cm (3/8 inch) wide strips with pastry wheel. Brush with beaten egg. Twist the strips and form into wreaths. Dip in the nuts and sugar. Place them on the baking sheet.

Bake on the center oven rack for around 10 minutes. Pictured on page 135.

PUFF PASTRY *(basic recipe)*

Puff pastry should be crispy and flaky.

4–4½ dl (1⅔–2 cups) all-purpose flour
1¼ dl (½ cup) water
1 teaspoon vinegar concentrate
200 g (¾ cup) margarine

▶ All ingredients should be at the same temperature – very cold.

Make a mound of most of the flour. Add the water and vinegar. Dice the margarine and cut just under ¼ of it into the other ingredients. Mix lightly, kneading as little as possible. Form into a round ball. Wrap in plastic and refrigerate for 15 minutes.

Cut a deep X into the dough. Sprinkle flour on the work surface. Roll into a 20 cm (8 inch) square. With a knife, draw a square on the diagonal (so that it looks like a diamond) within the square, cutting across the corners of the dough. Slice the margarine and arrange on the center square of dough. Fold the dough corners to the center, forming an envelope over the margarine (see pictures below). Turn the dough over, placing the seams against the work surface.

Carefully roll the dough, sprinkling lightly with flour as needed to prevent sticking, into a 30 cm (12 inch) square. Fold into thirds like a business letter. Roll out again and fold into thirds from the other direction. Wrap in plastic and refrigerate for at least 15 minutes.

Roll the dough into a square, a little larger than the previous one. Fold into thirds from one direction. Roll out again and fold into thirds from the other direction. Wrap in plastic and refrigerate for 15 minutes. Repeat one more time.

Now the dough is ready to shape.

Note: Frozen puff pastry can be used in all the following recipes.

Tips

When rolling out, place leftover bits on top of each other.

Never knead puff pastry.

Always place puff pastry on a fat-free baking sheet, preferably one that has been rinsed with cold water. Do not use a non-stick baking sheet.

Let the finished dough rest on the baking sheet for at least 10 minutes before baking. That helps the pastry to retain its shape.

Bake puff pastry on the center oven rack. Time and temperature depend on the thickness of the pastry.

Fold the dough to look like an envelope. Turn over.

Roll or flatten the dough. Fold into thirds.

Roll or flatten the dough. Fold it into thirds from the other direction.

PUFF PASTRY COMBS *25 pastries*

■ *Oven temperature 200–225 °C (400–425 °F), convection 200 °C (400 °F)*

1 batch Puff Pastry, see page 137

Brushing and garnish:
egg white
pearl sugar

▶ Prepare the puff pastry.

Roll into a 20 × 36 cm (10 × 15") sheet. Cut into rectangular pieces, 4 × 12 cm (2 × 5 inches). Make 3–4 cuts along one long side of each pastry, but do not cut all the way to the top. Brush with egg white and dip the tops in pearl sugar. Place the combs on a rinsed baking sheet. Bend the combs slightly and let them rest on the sheet for at least 10 minutes.

Bake on the center oven rack for around 12 minutes.

It is important to bake puff pastry until completely cooked. Otherwise, the pastry will fall and the baked goods will be chewy.

CHRISTMAS STARS *10 pastries*

■ *Oven temp: 200–225 °C (400–425 °F), convection 200 °C (400 °F)*

½ batch Puff Pastry, see page 137

Filling:
red currant jelly or preserves
Garnish:
powdered sugar
water

▶ Prepare the puff pastry.

Roll into a 18 × 45 cm (7 × 18 inch) sheet. Cut into 10 pieces of equal size.

Slit the corners toward the center but not all the way up. Place a spoonful of jelly or preserves in the center and twist every other corner toward the center. Press down. Place on cold, rinsed baking sheets. Let them rest on the sheets for at least 15 minutes.

Bake on the center oven rack for around 12 minutes.

When cool, drizzle with glaze made from powdered sugar mixed with a little water, or sift powdered sugar over.

Pictured on page 121.

PALMIERS *around 15 pastries*

■ *Oven temp: 225–250 °C (425–450 °F), convection 200 °C (400 °F)*

1 batch Puff Pastry, see page 137
sugar

▶ Prepare the puff pastry.

Sprinkle a thin layer of sugar over the work surface. Roll the dough into a 25 × 35 cm (10 × 14 inch) sheet. Sprinkle sugar over every surface of the dough. Fold the long sides to meet in the center. Sprinkle with sugar. Fold the dough double so that the short sides meet, and then once more lengthwise. Sprinkle with sugar between the folds, if necessary. Wrap in plastic and refrigerate until hard.

Cut the dough into 1 cm (3/8 inch) slices. Place on parchment-lined sheets.

Bake on the center oven rack for around 8 minutes. Turn and bake for around 5 minutes on the other side.

These palmiers also can be sandwiched with a little applesauce in between.

CONGRESS TARTS *25 pastries*

These are related to Polynesians, but with a flaky crust and a coarse filling.

■ *Oven temp: 175°C (350°F), convection 175°C (350°F)*
⅔ batch Puff Pastry, see page 137

Filling:
3 eggs
2 dl (¾ cup) sugar
200 g (1¾ cups) chopped hazelnuts or almonds.

▶ Prepare the puff pastry.

Roll into a thin sheet and press into individual tins, preferably oval. Prick the insides with a fork.

Beat the eggs and sugar lightly. Stir in the nuts and spoon into the pastry-lined tins.

Bake on a low oven rack for around 25 minutes.

Remove from the pans while still warm.

CATALANS *around 10 pastries*

■ *Oven temp: 175°C (350°F), 175°C (350°F)*
½ batch Puff Pastry, see page 137

Filling:
75 g (2½ ounces) almond paste
2 tablespoons stick margarine or butter
1 egg
1 tablespoon all-purpose flour

Garnish:
½ dl (3 tablespoons) raspberry preserves
1½ dl (⅔ cup) sifted powdered sugar

▶ Prepare the puff pastry.

Roll into a 18 × 45 cm (7 × 18 inch) sheet. Cut into 10 pieces of equal size and place in individual foil cups. Let rest while preparing the filling.

Grate the almond paste. Beat the butter, add the almond paste and the remaining ingredients.

Spoon the filling into the pastry-lined cups. Place on a baking sheet. Bake on a low oven rack for around 20 minutes. Leave in the cups.

Beat the preserves and sugar until smooth. Spread the glaze over the pastries. Refrigerate until the glaze has set.

ZOLA PASTRIES *10 pastries*

■ Oven temp: 250 °C (450 °F),
  convection 200 °C (400 °F)

1 batch Puff Pastry, see page 137

Filling:

5 gelatin sheets
2 dl (¾ cup) light cream
1 egg
1 egg yolk
2 tablespoons sugar
1 teaspoon vanilla
3 dl (1 cup) whipping cream

Glaze:

2 dl (¾ cup) sifted powdered sugar
1 ½ tablespoons water
1–2 teaspoons arrak extract or other
  flavoring

▶ Prepare the puff pastry.

Roll into a 36 × 22 cm (14 × 9 inch) sheet.
Cut it crosswise into 4 equal parts.

Place the pastry on a rinsed baking sheet.
Prick the sheets with a fork. Let them rest
for at least 15 minutes.

Bake on the center oven rack for around 6
minutes. Let cool.

Soak the gelatin in cold water for at least
5 minutes.

Combine the cream, egg, egg yolk and
sugar in a saucepan. Simmer, whisking constantly, until slightly thickened. Squeeze excess water from the gelatin and add, stirring
to melt. Let cool, stirring occasionally so
that it thickens evenly. Stir in the vanilla.

Whip the cream and fold into the cooked
cream.

Beat the sugar and water until smooth.
Flavor with arrak extract.

Spread the filling over 2 puff pastry
sheets. Top with the other two. Spread the
glaze over the top. Saw each carefully with a
sharp knife into 5 pieces.

ZOLA TORTE *12 servings*

Prepare the above recipe, but divide the
dough in half. Roll each piece into a 25 cm
(10 inch) square sheet. Prick with a fork. Let
rest for at least 15 minutes.

Bake for 8–10 minutes.

Spread cream over one puff pastry sheet.
Top with the other and spread with the
glaze.

NAPOLEONS *10 pastries*

■ *Oven temp: 225 °C (425 °F),*
convection 200 °C (400 °F)

1 batch Puff Pastry, see page 137

Filling:
2 ½ dl (1 cup) vanilla pastry cream or vanilla
pudding
1 dl (½ cup) whipping cream
1 ½ dl (⅔ cup) applesauce

Garnish:
2–3 tablespoons red currant jelly
1 dl (⅓ cup) sifted powdered sugar
1 tablespoon water

▶ Prepare the puff pastry.

Roll into a 24 × 40 cm (10 × 16 inch) sheet. Cut into 3 equal parts lengthwise.

Place on a rinsed baking sheet and prick with a fork. Let rest for at least 15 minutes.

Bake on the center oven rack for around 10 minutes. Let cool.

Beat the vanilla cream or pudding until smooth. Whip the cream and fold into the pudding.

Spread the applesauce on one of the pastry sheets. Top with a second sheet. Spread with vanilla cream. Top with the remaining sheet. Place with the underside up for easier spreading. Melt the jelly and spread a thin layer over the top layer of pastry. Beat the sugar and water until smooth. Spread over the jelly. Cut into 10 pieces of equal size. Serve immediately.

HOLSTEINS *12 pastries*

☆ This recipe won a prize in 1984.

■ *Oven temp: 150 °C (300 °F),*
convection 150 °C (300 °F)

3 egg whites
1 apple
150 g (1 ¼ cups) ground nuts
2 ½ dl (1 cup) sifted powdered sugar

Garnish:
1 dl (½ cup) whipping cream
1 dl (½ cup) thick blackberry preserves

▶ Grease a 12 muffin tin.

Beat the egg whites until stiff. Peel and coarsely grate the apple. Fold the apple shreds, nuts and sugar into the egg whites. Pour into the tin.

Bake on a low oven rack for around 45 minutes.

Remove from the pan.

Whip the cream. Pipe a ring around the edge of the cakes and down the sides, if desired. Top with preserves.

CHOCOLATE MACAROON CREAM CAKES *approx. 30*

■ *Oven temp: 175°C (350°F), convection 175°C (350°F)*

100 g (1 cup) ground almonds
1½ dl (⅔ cup) sugar
1–2 egg whites
or 150 g (5 ounces almond paste)
½ egg white

Filling:

150 g (⅔ cup) stick margarine or butter, softened
2 dl (¾ cup) vanilla pastry cream or vanilla pudding
1½ teaspoons vanilla
2 tablespoons powdered sugar
1 tablespoon cocoa

Garnish:

200 g (7 ounces) semi-sweet chocolate
25 g (2 tablespoons) coconut fat or 1 tablespoon vegetable oil

▶ Grease or line a baking sheet with parchment paper.

Combine the almonds and sugar. Lightly beat the egg whites. Fold into the almond mixture. Or grate the almond paste and beat with the egg white until smooth. Make small mounds of the mixture on the prepared sheet.

Bake on the center oven rack for around 8 minutes.

Remove from the sheet while warm. Let cool completely.

Beat the butter until fluffy. Gradually add the pastry cream and the remaining ingredients, beating until smooth.

Make a mound of the cream on the underside of the cookies. Refrigerate.

Melt the chocolate with the coconut fat or oil, see page 122. Dip the filled side of the cookies into the chocolate or brush it over the buttercream. Refrigerate until serving. Refrigerate any leftovers.

SARAH BERNHARDT CAKES
approx. 10 pastries

These are a more refined variation of the above cookies. Make these with almond paste.

■ *Oven temp: 150°C (300°F), convection 150°C (300°F)*

150 g (5 ounces) almond paste
½ egg white

Chocolate truffle filling:

75 g (3 ounces) semi-sweet chocolate
1 tablespoon butter
2 tablespoons whipping cream

Garnish:

200 g (7 ounces) semi-sweet chocolate
25 g (2 tablespoons) coconut fat or 1 tablespoon vegetable oil

▶ Grease or line a baking sheet with parchment paper.

Grate the almond paste. Lightly beat the egg white and beat into the almond paste. Make 10 mounds on the prepared sheet. Flatten with a floured hand.

Bake on the center oven rack for 12–14 minutes. Loosen from the sheet while still warm. Let cool upside down.

Melt the chocolate, see page 122. Heat the butter and cream to boiling. Whisk into the chocolate. Let cool until thick and stiff.

Spread the chocolate mixture over the cookies. Refrigerate for at least one hour.

Melt the chocolate with the oil, see page 122. Dip the cold cakes in the melted chocolate, covering the truffle filling completely.

GOTHENBURGERS

approx. 24 pastries

- *Oven temp: 200°C (400°F), convection 175°C (350°F)*

75 g (5 tablespoons) stick margarine or butter, softened
2 tablespoons sugar
½ egg
approx. 2 dl (¾ cup) all-purpose flour

Garnish (almond edge):
200 g (7 ounce) almond paste
1 egg white

Filling (mazarin mixture):
100 g (4 ounces) almond paste
50 g (3 tablespoons) stick margarine or butter, softened
1 egg, lightly beaten

Garnish:
red currant jelly or raspberry jelly
¾ dl (⅓ cup) sifted powdered sugar
2–3 teaspoons water
75 g (3 ounces) semi-sweet chocolate

▶ Combine the butter, sugar, egg and most of the flour in a food processor, pulsing until the dough begins to form a ball. Wrap in plastic and refrigerate for 30 minutes.

Grate the almond paste for the edge and beat with the egg white until smooth.

Grate the almond paste for the filling. Beat the butter until fluffy. Add the almond paste and the egg, a little at a time.

Roll out the pastry. Cut out 12 round cookies, around 9 cm (3 ¾ inches) in diameter. Place on a parchment-lined baking sheet. Spread the filling over the cakes, leaving a narrow edge bare.

Pipe the almond paste around the edge.

Bake on the center oven rack for 10–12 minutes. Let cool on a rack.

Spread a little jelly or preserves over the center of the cookies. Beat the powdered sugar and water until smooth and spread over the cookies. Divide into half-moons.

Melt the chocolate in a water bath or microwave oven. Dip the straight edge of the cookies in the chocolate. Let set.

FRAGILITES *12 pastries*

☆ This recipe won a prize in 1965.

■ *Oven temp: 175°C (350°F),*
  convection 175°C (350°F)

50 g (⅓ cup) ground almonds
2 dl (¾ cup) sugar
1 ½ tablespoons all-purpose flour
4 egg whites

Filling:
½ dl (¼ cup) all-purpose flour
1 ¼ dl (½ cup) water
1 egg yolk
150 g (⅔ cup) stick margarine or butter,
  softened
1 dl (½ cup) sifted powdered sugar
1 tablespoon vanilla sugar or 1 ½ teaspoons
  vanilla extract

Garnish: 50 g (2 ounces) semi-
sweet chocolate
powdered sugar
  (optional)

▶ Grease and flour a baking sheet.

Combine the almonds, sugar and flour. Beat the egg whites until stiff and fold into the nut mixture. Spread the batter into three lengths, 8 × 36 cm (3 × 14 inches).

Bake on the center or lower oven rack until dry and light, around 20 minutes.

Whisk the flour and water in a saucepan and heat to boiling, stirring constantly. Remove from the heat, whisk in the egg yolk and let rest for a few minutes. Beat the butter with the sugar and vanilla. Gradually add the cream. Beat well, preferably with an electric mixer until light and fluffy. Sandwich the almond pastries with the cream.

Melt the chocolate, see page 122. Spoon into a small plastic bag and cut a small hole in one quarter. Drizzle chocolate over the pastries. Sift over powdered sugar.

Cut the lengths into 3 cm (1 ¼ inch) pieces with a sharp knife. Refrigerate until serving time. Refrigerate any leftovers.

PUNCH PASTRIES *10–12 pastries*

☆ This recipe won a price in 1984.

■ *Oven temp: 175°C (350°F),*
  convection 175°C (350°F)

1 egg
2 egg yolks
4 tablespoons (¼ cup) sugar
4 tablespoons (¼ cup) potato starch or cornstarch
2 egg whites

Glaze:
2 ½ dl (1 cup) sifted powdered sugar
2 ½ tablespoons Swedish "Punsch" (or other
  liqueur)

Filling:
3 dl (1 cup) whipping cream

▶ Beat the egg, egg yolks and sugar until light yellow and very thick. Add the starch. Beat the egg whites until stiff and fold into the egg mixture.

Spoon the batter into 20–24 small rounds on a greased or parchment-lined baking sheet. The finished cookies should be 6 cm (2 ¼ inches) in diameter.

Bake on the center oven rack for 5–6 minutes, until light golden. Note! These rise in the oven and then fall when they hit room temperature. Let cool.

Remove a strip on each cookie to make a flat surface. Beat the powdered sugar with the punch. Spread over the "right" side.

Whip the cream and spoon into a pastry bag. Place the cookies two and two in paper cups with the unglazed surfaces facing and the straight edge at the bottom. Pipe cream between the cookies.

BIRGIT'S FAVORITES *10 pastries*

■ *Oven temp: 125°C (250°F), convection 125°C (250°F)*

Meringue shells:
3 egg whites
2 dl (¾ cup) sugar
Chocolate buttercream:
¾ dl (⅓ cup) sugar
¾ dl (⅓ cup) water
50 g (2 ounces) semi-sweet chocolate
3 egg yolks
150 g (⅔ cup) stick margarine or butter, softened
100 g (3 ounces) white chocolate
Filling:
3 dl (1 cup) whipping cream

▶ Combine the egg whites and sugar in a clean, dry bowl. Beat over a water bath until thick and glossy. A spoonful should retain a stiff peak. Divide the mixture among 20 individual foil cups. Place on a baking sheet.

Bake on a low oven rack for around 50 minutes. They should still be soft inside. Let cool.

For the buttercream, simmer the sugar and water until syrupy. It is ready when a sample forms a thread when rolled between two fingers.

Melt the semi-sweet chocolate.

Whisk the egg yolks. Gradually whisk in the syrup in a thin stream. Refrigerate.

Beat the butter until fluffy. Whisk in the egg cream by the spoonful. Whisk in the melted chocolate.

Whip the cream. Remove the meringue shells from the foil. Hollow out the centers. Sandwich the meringue shells with whipped cream. Spread the chocolate buttercream over the meringue shells, but do not cover completely. Grate the white chocolate and sprinkle over the pastries. Refrigerate until serving time. Refrigerate any leftovers.

Also pictured on page 121.

MOCHA PASTRIES
See page 168.

INDIVIDUAL PRINCESS CAKES
See page 159.

CREAM PUFFS *15 puffs*

These can be made entirely without sugar.

- ■ *Oven temp: 200°C (400°F),*
  convection 175°C (350°F)

3 dl (1 ¼ cups) water

100 g (7 tablespoons) stick margarine or butter

2 dl (¾ cup + 2 tablespoons) all-purpose flour

3 medium eggs

Filling:

2 ½ dl (1 cup) whipping cream

vanilla

Garnish:

powdered sugar, water and cocoa (optional)

▶ Grease or line a baking sheet with parchment paper.

Heat the water and butter to boiling. Stir in the flour. Let simmer, beating constantly, until the mixture pulls away from the sides of the pan.

Remove from the heat and let cool. Add the eggs, one at a time, beating well after each. Spoon onto the prepared sheet or fill a pastry bag and pipe out desired shapes.

Bake on a lower oven rack for around 20 minutes. Do not open the oven door during the first 10 minutes. Cream puffs are very sensitive to drafts.

Remove from the oven and let cool.

Whip the cream until very stiff. Flavor with vanilla.

Cut a lid on each puff, or make a hole in the side. Fill with cream. Sift powdered sugar over or beat powdered sugar with water (and cocoa, if desired) until smooth and drizzle or spread over the puffs.

Fresh or frozen berries can be mixed into the cream.

Vanilla and chocolate pastry cream are good fillings for cream puffs.

Cream Puffs

Maria Buns

MARIA BUNS *15 pastries*

These are also called Tea Buns.

- *Oven temp: 175°C (350°F), convection 175°C (350°F)*

2 dl (¾ cup) all-purpose flour
3 tablespoons sugar
75 g (5 tablespoons) cold stick margarine or butter
1 batch Cream Puff pastry

Filling:
2 egg yolks
1 tablespoon sugar
1 tablespoon potato starch or cornstarch
3 dl (1 cup) light cream
1 tablespoon vanilla sugar or 1½ teaspoons vanilla extract
1 dl (½ cup) whipping cream

Garnish:
powdered sugar

▶ Grease or line a baking sheet with parchment paper.

Combine the flour and sugar. Dice the butter and cut it into the dry ingredients, kneading lightly. Wrap in plastic and refrigerate for at least an hour.

Prepare the cream puff pastry. Spoon mounds, far apart, on the prepared sheet.

Roll the butter cookie dough to a 3 mm (¼ inch) thick sheet. Cut out 6 cm (2 ¼ inch) circles. Place one cookie on each cream puff mound.

Bake on a lower oven rack for 40–45 minutes, until they feel very light. Let cool.

Combine the egg yolks, sugar, starch and cream in a saucepan. Simmer, whisking constantly, until thickened. Let cool slightly, then stir in the vanilla. Refrigerate until cold.

Whip the cream and carefully fold it into the pastry cream.

Make a hole in the bottom of each bun and fill with the cream. Sift powdered sugar over.

FILLED CREAM PUFF WREATH
12–15 servings

- *Oven temp: 200°C (400°F), convection 175°C (350°F)*

1 batch Cream Puff pastry

Filling:
3 dl (1 cup) whipping cream
fruit or berries

Garnish:
1 ½ dl (⅔ cup) powdered sugar
1–2 tablespoons water
25 g (¼ cup) sliced almonds

▶ Draw a 20 cm (8 inch) circle on baking parchment. Grease and flour.

Prepare the cream puff pastry. Spoon mounds in a wreath or pipe a thick wreath around the circle.

Bake on a low oven rack for around 25 minutes. Lower the temperature to 150°C (300°F). Bake for 10–15 minutes more with the oven door slightly open. Remove the pastry from the oven. Turn off the heat. Make a few holes in the wreath. Return to the oven and let dry for around 10 minutes with the door slightly open.

Whip the cream until very stiff. Divide the wreath in half horizontally. Fold fruit or berries into the cream and spoon into the bottom half. Top with the remaining half.

Beat the sugar and water until smooth. Spread it over the wreath. Sprinkle with sliced almonds, toasted, if desired.

WALES PASTRY *20 servings*

- Oven temp: 200°C (400°F),
  convection 175°C (350°F)

150 g (⅔ cup) cold stick margarine or butter
2½ dl (1 cup) all-purpose flour
3 tablespoons water
1 batch Cream Puff pastry, see page 146

Garnish:
3 dl (1¼ cups) sifted powdered sugar
2 tablespoons water
1 tablespoon red currant jelly
50 g (½ cup) sliced almonds

▶ Grease or line a baking sheet with parchment paper.

Dice the butter and place it with the flour in a food processor. Pulse until crumbly. Add the water and pulse until the dough forms a ball. Wrap in plastic and refrigerate for a while.

Prepare the cream puff pastry.

Divide the pie crust dough in half. Roll each into an 8 × 30 cm (3 × 12 inch) rectangle. Place on the baking sheet and prick with a fork. Pipe the cream puff pastry in a zig-zag pattern onto the dough rectangles.

Bake on a low oven rack for 25 minutes, until dry and light. Transfer to a rack.

Beat the sugar, water and jelly until smooth. Toast the almonds lightly in the oven. Spread the glaze over the pastry. Sprinkle with almonds. Let dry. Cut each length into 10 pieces.

Vanilla cream or whipped cream are good fillings for this pastry.

FLAKY KNOTS *around 12 pastries*

- Oven temp: 200°C (400°F),
  convection 175°C (350°F)

1 batch Cream Puff pastry, see page 146
300 g (10 ounces) puff pastry

Filling:
2 eggs
1 dl (⅓ cup) sugar
grated zest and juice of 1–2 lemons
50 g (3 tablespoons) stick margarine or butter
3 dl (1 cup) whipping cream

Garnish:
2 dl (¾ cup) sifted powdered sugar
1½–2 tablespoons lemon juice and water

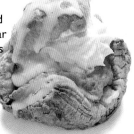

▶ Prepare the cream puff pastry.

Roll out the puff pastry and cut into 12 squares of equal size.

Spoon mounds of cream puff pastry onto each puff pastry square. Turn up the corners on each square.

Bake for 45–50 minutes. Let cool completely.

Beat the eggs and sugar in a saucepan. Whisk in the lemon zest and juice. Simmer, whisking constantly, until thickened. Let cool for a few minutes, then beat in the butter in pats. Refrigerate until very cold. Whip the cream.

Carefully cut an opening on one side of the cream puff part. Fill with lemon cream and whipped cream.

Beat the sugar and juice until smooth and drizzle over the pastries.

The filling and decorations make the cake

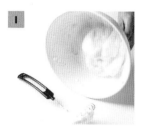

Beat the egg whites until stiff. Use a clean, dry round-bottomed bowl. A few grains of salt or a drop of vinegar concentrate produce a stiffer mass. Beat slowly at first, then quickly. The beaten egg whites should form stiff peaks and stay in place when the bowl is turned upside down.

Soft butter. Buttercream is easier to prepare with soft butter or margarine. Remove the butter from the refrigerator early enough for it to soften. Or slice with a cheese plane into a bowl. Butter can also be softened in the microwave oven.

Protect the cake platter. Tear parchment paper into 3–4 strips. Place them under the unfrosted cake. Carefully remove them when the cake is ready to serve.

Pattern with a fork. The fork is invaluable as a garnishing tool. It can be used to make patterns in buttercream, whipped cream or frosting.

Cones. If you don't have a pastry bag with a removable tip, you can make one from parchment paper. Fold a piece of parchment paper in half. Roll one corner in toward the middle so that the pointed tip is on the long side of the paper. Roll over the other corner and fasten with a paper clip. Cut off the pointed tip. You can also use a plastic bag.

Rolling marzipan. Roll marzipan between two sheets of plastic wrap to prevent it from sticking. Remove one piece of plastic and drape the marzipan over the cake. Arrange it evenly, then remove the remaining plastic. Trim excess marzipan.

7 **Flowers and leaves.** Tint marzipan light pink or yellow with food coloring.

Flowers: Make a narrow roll around 25 cm (10 inches) long and place it on the work surface. Pull out the marzipan roll with a small spatula to form petals. Carefully lift up the entire length and roll into a flower. Or make balls in different sizes and shape them into petals with your fingers. Gather together to form a rose.

Leaves. Roll out the marzipan and cut leaves with a knife. Or make balls and flatten them into leaves.

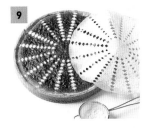

Glazing and decorating. Make a sugar glaze from powdered sugar and water and spread it over the cold cake or pastry.

Decorating jelly should be squeezed through a small paper or plastic bag with one corner cut off. Or use a wooden pick to apply the jelly and make a pattern with it.

Decorate with sugar. Fold a piece of parchment paper in half and cut out a pattern. Or use a purchased stencil. Sift powdered sugar over to make a design on the cake.

AMBROSIA CAKE *12 servings*

☆ This recipe won a prize in 1965.

- Oven temp: *150°C (300°F),*
  convection 150°C (350°F)

125 g (½ cup) butter or stick margarine
2 eggs
1 ½ dl (⅔ cup) sugar
1 ½ dl (⅔ cup) all-purpose flour
½ teaspoon baking powder

Glaze:
3 dl (1 ¼ cups) sifted powdered sugar
2–3 tablespoons water
  or orange or lemon juice
4 tablespoons (¼ cup) diced candied orange
  peel

▶ Grease and flour a 25 cm (10 inch) round cake pan.

Melt the butter and let it cool.

Beat the eggs and sugar until light yellow and very thick. Add the flour, baking powder and melted butter, mixing well. Pour into the prepared pan.

Bake on a lower oven rack for around 25 minutes.

Let cool for at least 5 minutes, then remove from the pan. Let cool on a rack.

Beat the powdered sugar and water or juice until smooth. Spread over the cake. Sprinkle with orange peel.

ALMOND-LEMON CAKE *12 servings*

- Oven temp: *175°C (350°F), convection*
  175°C (350°F)

150 g (⅔ cup) butter, softened
3 dl (1 ¼ cups) sugar
2 large eggs
grated zest of 1 large lemon
1 dl (⅓ cup) milk
4 dl (1 ⅔ cups) all-purpose flour
2 teaspoons baking powder

Glaze:
green food coloring
50 g (½ cup) chopped almonds
2–3 dl (¾–1 ¼ cups) sifted powdered sugar
2–3 tablespoons lemon juice

▶ Grease and flour a 24 cm (10 inch) round cake pan.

Beat the butter and sugar until light and fluffy. Add the eggs, one at a time, beating well after each. Add the lemon zest and milk. Combine the dry ingredients and add, mixing well. Pour into the prepared pan.

Ambrosia Cake

Bake on a lower oven rack for 35–40 minutes, until a cake tester comes out dry.

Tint the almonds green. Beat the powdered sugar and lemon juice until smooth. Spread over the cake while still warm. Sprinkle with almonds.

Before glazing, the cake can be split horizontally and filled with lemon cream, see Little Lemon Tarts, page 130. Mix the lemon cream with whipped cream, if desired.

TOSCA CAKE *16 servings*

■ *Oven temp: 175 °C (350 °F), convection 175 °C (350 °F)*
100 g (7 tablespoons) stick margarine or butter
2 large eggs
1 ½ dl (¾ cup) sugar
2 dl (1 cup) all-purpose flour
1 teaspoon baking powder
½ dl (¼ cup) light cream or milk

Topping:
100 g (7 tablespoons) butter or margarine
1 dl (½ cup) sugar
2 tablespoons all-purpose flour
2 tablespoons milk
100 g (¾ cup) slivered almonds

▶ Grease and flour a 24 cm (10 inch) springform pan.

Melt the butter and let it cool. Beat the eggs and sugar until light yellow and very thick. Combine the dry ingredients and add alternately with the milk and melted butter, mixing well. Pour into the prepared pan.

Bake on a lower oven rack for 20–25 minutes. Prepare the topping while the cake is baking.

Combine all the ingredients in a saucepan. Heat, stirring carefully, until thickened. Spread over the cake. Move the cake to the center of the oven. Bake for 15 minutes more, until golden and bubbly.

Lemon Almond Cake

Tosca Cake

LINZER TORTE *16 servings*

■ *Oven temp: 175°C (350°F),*
convection 150°C (300°F)

200 g (¾ cup) butter
1½ dl (⅔ cup) sugar
3 eggs
½ teaspoon ground cloves
1 teaspoon cinnamon
200 g (2½ cups) ground hazelnuts
2 dl (¾ cup) fine breadcrumbs
2 dl (¾ cup) thick raspberry preserves
powdered sugar

▶ Grease a 24 cm (10 inch) springform pan.

Beat the butter and sugar until light and fluffy. Add the eggs, one at a time, beating well after each. Stir in the spices, nuts and breadcrumbs.

Spread ⅔ of the cake mixture into the pan, a little higher around the edge. Top with the preserves. Spoon the remaining cake mixture into a pastry bag with a plain tip. Pipe a lattice over the cake.

Bake on a lower oven rack for around 45 minutes. Cover with aluminum foil after 30 minutes, so the cake won't get too dark.

This torte tastes even better if allowed to mature for a few days.

Sift powdered sugar over just before serving.

APPLE TORTE *16 servings*

■ *Oven temp: 175°C (350°F),*
convection 175°C (350°F)

100 g (7 tablespoons) cold stick margarine
or butter
2 dl (¾ cup) all-purpose flour
2 tablespoons sugar
1 egg yolk
Filling:
200 g (7 ounces) almond paste
1 egg
3 apples (around 500g/1 lb)
1 teaspoon cinnamon
1 tablespoon sugar
Topping and glaze:
400 g (14 ounces) almond paste
1–2 egg whites
1 dl (⅓ cup) water
1 dl (⅓ cup) sugar
pinch citric or ascorbic acid

▶ Grease a 24 cm (10 inch) springform pan.

Dice the butter and place in a food processor with the flour and sugar. Pulse until crumbly. Add the egg yolk and pulse until the mixture starts to form a ball. Wrap in plastic and refrigerate for at least an hour.

Press the dough into the pan. Bake on a lower oven rack for around 10 minutes.

Grate the almond paste and beat with the egg until smooth. Spread over the crust. Peel, slice and toss apples with sugar and cinnamon. Spread over the almond paste layer.

Grate the almond paste. Beat in the egg whites until smooth. Spoon into a pastry bag with a plain tip and pipe over the apples.

Bake for 30–35 minutes. Let cool.

Simmer the water and sugar until syrupy. Add the acid. Let it cool. Brush over the torte.

WHIPPED CREAM TORTE
20 servings

This classic can be varied with different kinds of fruit and berries.

■ *Oven temp: 175°C (350°F), convection 175°C (350°F)*

Sponge cake base:
4 large eggs
2 dl (1 cup) sugar
1 dl (½ cup) all-purpose flour
¾ dl (⅓ cup) potato starch or cornstarch
1½ teaspoons baking powder

Filling and garnish:
5 dl (2 cups) whipping cream

Berries and fruit, such as:
• strawberries and banana or pineapple
• physalis, mango, papaya, carambola, grapes
• blackberries, raspberries, strawberries or wild strawberries
• raspberries and blueberries
walnuts or chopped nuts
or grated chocolate

▶ Grease and flour a 26 cm (10 inch) springform pan.

Beat the eggs and sugar until light yellow and very thick. Combine the dry ingredients and fold into the egg mixture. Pour into the prepared pan.

Bake on a lower oven rack for around 40 minutes.

Let cool for 10 minutes, then remove from the pan. When completely cold, divide horizontally into 3 layers.

Whip all the cream. Reserve just under half for garnishing. Spread whipped cream over two layers and top with fruit. Stack, ending with the plain top layer. Cover the entire cake with whipped cream. Garnish with fruit and/or berries, nuts or grated chocolate.

Pictured on page 149.

JELLIED FRUIT TORTE *20 servings*

■ *Oven temp: 175°C (350°F), convection 175°C (350°F)*

1 sponge cake base, see Whipped Cream Torte

Filling 1:
3 egg yolks
1½ tablespoons potato starch or cornstarch
1½ tablespoons sugar
3 dl (1 cup) whipping cream
1 tablespoon vanilla sugar or 1½ teaspoons vanilla extract

Filling 2:
1–1½ dl (½ cup) fruit preserves or puree

Garnish:
50 g (½ cup) sliced almonds
fresh fruit or well-drained canned fruit

Jelly:
6 gelatin sheets
2½ dl (1 cup) water
3–4 tablespoons sugar
½ teaspoon citric or ascorbic acid

▶ Bake the sponge cake base according to the previous recipe. When completely cold, divide horizontally into three layers.

For filling 1, combine all ingredients except the vanilla in a saucepan and simmer, stirring constantly, until thickened. Let it cool. Stir in the vanilla.

For the jelly, soak the gelatin in cold water for at least 5 minutes. Heat the water, sugar and citric acid to boiling. Melt the gelatin in the hot liquid. Let cool until partially set.

Spread ⅔ of the vanilla cream on the bottom layer. Top with the second layer and spread with fruit preserves or puree. Cover with the third layer. Spread the remaining vanilla cream over the puree and around the edge of the torte.

Sprinkle the nuts around the sides of the cake. Top with fruit. Spoon the partially set jelly over the fruit. Refrigerate until set.

Pictured on page 149.

PRINCESS TORTE *approx. 20 servings*

A Swedish classic.

■ *Oven temp: 175°C (350°F),*
  convection 175°C (350°F)

4 eggs
2 dl (1 cup) sugar
1 dl (½ cup) all-purpose flour
1 dl (½ cup) potato starch or cornstarch
2 teaspoons baking powder

Filling:
4 gelatin sheets
2 dl (1 cup) vanilla pastry cream (see recipe
  for Vanilla Hearts, page 130)
3 dl (1 cup) whipping cream
2 teaspoons vanilla sugar or 1 teaspoon
  vanilla extract

Garnish:
300 g (10 ounces) marzipan
green food coloring
powdered sugar

▶ Grease and flour a 26 cm (10 inch) spring-form pan.

Beat the eggs and sugar until light yellow and very thick. Combine the dry ingredients and fold into the egg mixture. Pour into the prepared pan.

Bake on a lower oven rack for around 40 minutes.

Let cool for at least 5 minutes, then remove from the pan.

Soak the gelatin in cold water for at least 5 minutes.

Prepare the vanilla cream. While it is still hot, add the gelatin, stirring to melt.

Whip the cream. Fold into the vanilla cream when it begins to thicken. Stir in the vanilla. Let the cream partially set.

When completely cold, divide the cake horizontally into 3 layers. The top layer should be just under 1 cm (3/8 inch) thick. Spread most of the cream filling on the bottom two layers, mounding it a little higher toward the center, so that the cake will be rounded on top. Stack, ending with the thin top layer. Spread the remaining cream over the top and sides of the cake.

Tint the marzipan and roll into a thin, smooth sheet. It should be large enough to cover the cake completely, even the sides. Roll it up on a rolling pin and carefully unroll over the cake without forming pleats at the bottom. Cut off excess marzipan with a pastry wheel or knife.

Sift powdered sugar over.

STRAWBERRY COTTAGE CHEESE CAKE *approx. 18 servings*

This cake has a fresh flavor and appeals to those who prefer their desserts less sweet.

- *Oven temp: 175 °C (350 °F), convection 150 °C (300 °F)*

2 eggs
1 ½ dl (⅔ cup) sugar
1 ½ dl (⅔ cup) all-purpose flour
1 teaspoon baking powder

Filling:
7 gelatin sheets
3 egg yolks (pasteurised) or 3 ½ tablespoons egg substitute (refrigerated or defrosted)
1 dl (½ cup) sugar
grated zest and juice of ½ lemon
1 teaspoon vanilla
500 g (18 ounces) creamed cottage cheese
3 dl (1 cup) whipping cream
1 dl (⅓ cup) strawberry preserves

Garnish:
powdered sugar
25 g (¼ cup) sliced almonds

▶ Grease and flour a 22 cm (9 inch) spring-form pan.

Beat the eggs and sugar until light yellow and very thick. Fold in the dry ingredients. Pour into the prepared pan.

Bake on a lower oven rack for around 20 minutes.

Let cool for 5 minutes, then remove from the pan. When completely cold, divide horizontally into 2 layers.

Soak the gelatin in cold water for at least 5 minutes. Beat the egg yolks and sugar until light yellow and very thick. Add the lemon zest and juice and the vanilla. Press the cottage cheese through a sieve and stir into the egg yolk mixture. Whip the cream and fold into the egg yolk mixture.

Squeeze the excess water from the gelatin and melt in a small saucepan over low heat or in the microwave oven. Let cool slightly, then fold into the cottage cheese mixture.

Line the pan the cake was baked in with plastic wrap. Spread the cut side of both cake layers with preserves. Place one layer in the pan, strawberry side up. Fill with the cottage cheese mixture. Top with the second layer, strawberry side down. Refrigerate for at least 4 hours.

Remove the cake from the pan. Sift powdered sugar over and sprinkle sliced almonds around the sides of the cake.

CARAMEL TORTE *around 15 servings*

■ *Oven temp: 175°C (350°F),*
  convection 175°C (350°F)

300 g (10 ounces) almond paste
2 egg whites

Caramel cream:
3 dl (1 cup) whipping cream
2 dl (¾ cup) sugar
1 dl (⅓ cup) light corn syrup
1 tablespoon butter or margarine
2 teaspoons vanilla sugar or 1 teaspoon
  vanilla extract

Filling:
1 dl (½ cup) crème fraiche or dairy sour
  cream

Garnish: 50 g (½ cup) sliced almonds

▶ Grease and flour or line a baking sheet
with parchment paper. Draw two 18 × 20 cm
(7 × 8 inch) rectangles on the paper.

Coarsely grate the almond paste. Beat the
egg whites until stiff. Combine. Spread the
mixture in an even layer over the rectangles.

Bake on the center oven rack for around
10 minutes. Remove from the baking sheet
and let cool.

Combine the cream, sugar and syrup in a
saucepan. Cook over medium heat for
30–40 minutes, until it becomes a thick,
golden brown cream. Stir in the butter and
let it cool. Stir in the vanilla.

Spread a thin layer of crème fraiche over
one cake layer and top with half the caramel
cream. Top with the other cake layer and
cover with the remaining cream. Lightly
toast the almonds and sprinkle over the cake.

This cake can be cut into 40 tiny petit
fours.

Pictured on page 163.

CAKE LOG *15 servings*

■ *Oven temp: 250°C (450°F),*
  convection 200°C (400°F)

3 eggs
1 ½ dl (⅔ cup) sugar
¾ dl (⅓ cup) potato starch or cornstarch
1 tablespoon all-purpose flour
1 teaspoon baking powder

Filling:
1 tablespoon butter
1 ½ dl (⅔ cup) water
2 tablespoons all-purpose flour
1 egg yolk
150 g (⅔ cup) butter or stick margarine,
  softened
1 dl (⅓ cup) sifted powdered sugar
1 teaspoon vanilla sugar or ½ teaspoon
  vanilla extract
¾ dl (⅓ cup) thick raspberry or strawberry
  preserves

Garnish:
250 g (9 ounces) marzipan
yellow food coloring
50 g (2 ounces) semi-sweet chocolate

▶ Line a 25 × 35 cm (10 × 15 inch) pan with
parchment paper.

Beat the eggs and sugar until light yellow
and very thick. Combine the dry ingredients
and fold into the egg mixture. Spread in the
prepared pan.

Bake on the center oven rack for around 5
minutes.

Turn the cake out onto parchment paper
sprinkled with sugar. Brush cold water over
the baking parchment so that it releases easily. Carefully remove the paper from the
cake and let it cool.

Combine the butter and water in a
saucepan. Add the flour and let simmer for a
few minutes. Whisk in the egg yolk and let
the cream cool.

Beat the butter and powdered sugar until
light and fluffy. Gradually add the cooked
cream, beating until smooth. Stir in the
vanilla.

Spread most of the buttercream over the cake. Make one or two strips of preserves across the cake. Roll up from the short side to form a stubby log. Trim the edges. Spread the remaining buttercream over the log. Press the cake down in a couple of places to make the log appear more realistic.

Tint the marzipan pale yellow. Roll into a thin rectangular sheet large enough to cover the log completely. Roll it up on a rolling pin and carefully unroll it over the cake.

Melt the chocolate, see page 122. Brush chocolate over the ends and in several places on the exterior to make it look natural.

INDIVIDUAL PRINCESS CAKES

10 cakes

- *Oven temp: 250 °C (450 °F), convection: 200 °C (400 °F)*

1 sponge cake base, see Cake Log

Filling:
1–1 ½ dl (½ – ⅔ cup) thick applesauce or preserves

Garnish:
300 g (10 ounces) marzipan
red food coloring
3 dl (1 cup) whipping cream
preserves or nuts (optional)

▶ Prepare the sponge cake base according to the previous recipe.

Spread with applesauce or preserves. Roll up lengthwise. Cut into 3 cm (1 ¼ inch) slices. Place cut side up.

Tint the marzipan light pink.

Whip the cream until very thick. Spread a little around the edge of each round of cake.

Roll the marzipan into a thin sheet. Cut strips 1 cm (⅜ inch) wider than the cake in height and length, so they are large enough. Pipe whipped cream in a spiral over each slice of cake. Garnish each with a spoonful of preserves or a nut half.

Pictured on page 121.

MOUSSE TORTE *12–14 servings*

■ *Oven temp: 175°C (350°F),*
   convection 175°C (350°F)

Sponge cake base:
3 eggs
1 ½ dl (⅔ cup) sugar
1 ½ dl (⅔ cup) all-purpose flour

Filling 1:
5 dl (2 cups) plucked red currants or
   raspberries

Filling 2:
500 g (18 ounces) farmer cheese or quark
   (10% fat)
9 gelatin sheets
grated zest and juice of 1 lemon
4 egg yolks (pasteurised) or 4 ½ tablespoons
   egg substitute (refrigerated or defrosted)
1 ½ dl (⅔ cup) sugar
1 ½ dl (⅔ cup) milk
5 dl (2 cups) whipping cream

Garnish:
3 gelatin sheets
3 dl (1 ¼ cups) strained red currant
   (or raspberry) juice
1–1 ½ dl (½–2/3) whipping cream
sugared red currants or raspberries

▶ Grease and flour a 24 cm (10 inch) spring-
form pan.

Beat the eggs and sugar until light yellow and very thick. Fold in the flour, mixing well. Pour into the prepared pan. Bake on a lower oven rack for around 20 minutes. Let cool in the pan.

Place the currants and sugar in a food processor or blender and puree. Strain off the juice and reserve.

Soak all gelatin (both for filling and garnish) in cold water for at least 5 minutes. Combine the lemon zest, 2 tablespoons juice, egg yolks, sugar and milk in a saucepan. Simmer over low heat, whisking constantly, until smooth and thick.

Remove from the heat and let cool for a few minutes. Squeeze excess water from 9 gelatin sheets and add to the lemon cream. Stir to melt. Place the pan in a bowl of cold water, stirring occasionally, to cool faster. Transfer to a bowl.

Remove the cake from the pan and divide in half horizontally. Let the lower half remain on the base of the pan.

Cut 2 strips of parchment paper, 15 × 20 cm (6 × 8 inches). Cover the bottom of the pan with the paper and reattach the sides.

Spread the fruit puree in an even layer over the bottom cake layer. Top with the second cake layer. Press down.

Press the farmer cheese through a sieve.

When the lemon cream begins to set, beat in the cheese. Whip the cream until thick but not too stiff and fold into the lemon cream. Pour over the cake in an even layer. Refrigerate for 3–4 hours.

Measure the strained juice and add additional red currant juice (available at health food stores) to make 3 dl (1 ¼ cups). Melt the remaining gelatin sheets over low heat or in a microwave oven. Let cool slightly. Pour into the juice in a thin stream. Spoon carefully over the filling to form a smooth mirror. Refrigerate until stiff.

Carefully remove the sides of the cake pan. Remove the paper strips. Transfer to a serving platter. Whip the remaining cream and pipe around the cake. Garnish with sugared currants or other berries.

TOFFEE CRUNCH TORTE
around 15 servings

A festive torte that can be kept frozen until serving time.

■ Oven temp: 150°C (300°F),
    convection 150°C (300°F)

Meringue:
100 g (1 cup) chopped nuts
3 egg whites
2 dl (¾ cup) sugar
1 liter (quart) good quality vanilla ice cream
4 individual chocolate toffee crunch bars
    (such as Dajm, Skor or Heath)
or 1 dl (½ cup) chopped almonds and
50 g (2 ounces) semi-sweet chocolate mini-chips

Garnish:
crushed chocolate toffee crunch bars and
    fruit or cocoa

▶ Grease and flour or line a baking sheet with parchment paper. Draw a 26 cm (10 inch) circle on the paper.

Toast the nuts in a dry, hot frying pan. Beat the egg whites until stiff. Gradually add the sugar and beat until thick and glossy. Stir in the nuts. Spread over the circle on the baking sheet.

Bake on the center oven rack for around 45 minutes. Let cool.

Let the ice cream soften slightly. Crush the candy bars and fold into the softened ice cream or fold in the almonds and mini-chips.

Make an aluminum foil ring around the meringue. It should extend a few centimeters (2 inches) over the meringue. Pour the ice cream mixture onto the meringue in an even layer, smoothing the top.

Freeze for at least 5 hours. Cover with foil if it is to be frozen for a longer period of time.

Decorate with crushed candy bars or fruit and sift cocoa over right before serving.

ZULEIKA TORTE 12–15 servings

■ Oven temp: 175°C (350°F),
   convection 175°C (350°F)
3 egg whites
100 g (1 cup) ground almonds
1 dl (½ cup) sugar

Garnish:
3 egg yolks
¾ dl (⅓ cup) sugar
2 dl (1 cup) whipping cream
50 g (3 tablespoons) butter, softened
25 g (¼ cup) sliced or chopped almonds

▶ Grease and flour a 24 cm (10 inch) round cake pan

Beat the egg whites until stiff. Combine the almonds and sugar. Carefully fold in the whites. Spread in the prepared pan.

Bake on a lower oven rack for around 25 minutes. Remove from the pan and let cool.

Whisk the egg yolks, sugar, cream and butter together in a saucepan. Simmer, whisking constantly, until thickened. Do not allow to boil or the eggs will scramble.

Let the cream cool slightly. Pour over the meringue base. Toast the almonds and sprinkle over the cake. Serve very cold.

For a fluffier cream: Whisk only half the cream into the egg yolk mixture. Whip the rest and fold into the cold pastry cream.

TIRAMISU 8–10 servings

An Italian sponge cake filled with mascarpone, an Italian fresh cream cheese.

■ Oven temp: 175°C (350°F),
   convection 175°C (350°F)

Sponge cake base:
4 eggs
2 dl (¾ cup) sugar
4 teaspoons instant coffee granules +
   1 tablespoon boiling water
1 dl (⅓ cup) potato starch or cornstarch
1 dl (½ cup) all-purpose flour
2 teaspoons baking powder

Filling:
5 gelatin sheets
1 tablespoon hot strong coffee
2 eggs (pasteurised) or 6 tablespoons egg
   substitute (refrigerated or defrosted)
1 dl (½ cup) sugar
200 g (7 ounces) mascarpone or light cream
   cheese
grated zest of 1 lemon
2 dl (1 cup) whipping cream
2 egg whites

Soaking:
½ dl (3 tablespoons) boiling water
½ dl (3 tablespoons) cognac
4 teaspoons instant coffee granules

Garnish:
cocoa

▶ Grease and flour a 24 cm (10 inch) round cake pan.

Beat the eggs and sugar until light yellow and very thick. Dissolve the coffee in the water and add. Combine the dry ingredients and fold into the egg mixture. Pour into the prepared pan.

Bake on a lower oven rack for around 35 minutes. Let cool for around 5 minutes, then remove from the pan and let cool on a rack.

Soak the gelatin in cold water for at least 5 minutes. Squeeze to remove excess water and melt in the hot coffee, stirring occasionally until dissolved. Beat the eggs and sugar until light yellow and very thick. Fold in the mascarpone and the lemon zest. Add the gelatin mixture in a thin stream, stirring lightly. Whip the cream and fold into the egg yolk mixture. Beat the egg whites until stiff and fold into the egg mixture. Freeze for around an hour.

Divide the cake horizontally into three layers. Combine the water, cognac and coffee and drizzle over the cake. Spread the egg cream over the two lower layers and top with the uppermost layer. Spread the remaining cream over the top and around the sides of the cake. Sift a thin layer of cocoa over the torte. Refrigerate until serving time. Refrigerate any leftovers.

From the top: Zuleika Torte,
page 162; Mazarin Torte, page
131; Tiramisu, page 162, and
Caramel Torte, page 158.

FRENCH CHOCOLATE CAKE

around 12 servings

■ *Oven temp: 200°C (400°F),*
  convection 200°C (400°F)

175 g (6 ounces) stick margarine or butter
175 g (6 ounces) semi-sweet or bittersweet
  chocolate
2 dl (¾ cup) sugar
3 eggs
1 ½ dl (⅔ cup) all-purpose flour
½ teaspoon instant coffee granules

Glaze:

1 dl (⅓ cup) whipping cream
150 g (5 ounces) semi-sweet or bittersweet
  chocolate
25 g (2 tablespoons) butter

▶ Grease and flour a 24 cm (10 inch) spring-form pan.

Melt the butter in a large saucepan. Remove from the heat. Break the chocolate into pieces and add, stirring occasionally to melt.

Stir in the sugar. Separate the eggs, reserving the whites in a large mixer bowl. Add the yolks to the chocolate mixture, beating with a hand mixer until light and fluffy. Combine the flour and coffee granules and add, mixing well. Beat the egg whites until stiff and fold into the chocolate mixture.

Pour into the prepared pan.

Bake immediately on the lowest oven rack for 25–30 minutes. The cake should still be a little moist in the center.

Loosen the sides of the pan and let the cake cool. The top may have cracked a little during baking.

Scald the cream. Break the chocolate into pieces and add with the butter. Stir until completely melted. Let the glaze cool a little. Pour over the cake and spread with a spatula.

Serve cold, preferably with whipped cream. This cake can also be glazed with melted chocolate and garnished with whipped cream.

MICRO-CHOCOLATE CAKE

approx. 12 servings

1 ½ dl (⅔ cup) sugar
2 dl (¾ cup) all-purpose flour
1 teaspoon baking powder
1 ½ tablespoons cocoa
75 g (5 tablespoons) butter or margarine
¾ dl (⅓ cup) water
2 small or 1 large egg

1 teaspoon vanilla sugar or ½ teaspoon
  vanilla extract
2 tablespoons chocolate sprinkles

▶ Combine the dry ingredients in a bowl.

Place the butter in a glass pie plate and melt at the highest setting.

Lightly beat the egg and stir it into the flour mixture. Add the melted butter and vanilla, mixing well. Pour the batter into the pie plate.

Bake on the medium setting for around 8 minutes. It can be a little sticky inside. Sprinkle the chocolate sprinkles over the warm cake and garnish with fruit, such as persimmons and grapes. Serve right from the pie plate with whipped cream alongside.

BUDAPEST ROLL 10–12 servings

■ Oven temp. 175°C (350°F), convection
  175°C (350°F)
5 egg whites
3 dl (1 ¼ cups) sugar
150 g (1 ⅓ cups) finely chopped nuts
1 dl (½ cup) all-purpose flour
2 tablespoons cocoa
50 g (½ cup) sliced almonds

Filling:
3 dl (1 cup) whipping cream
1 tin (300g/10 oz) mandarin oranges
Garnish:
powdered sugar

▶ Line a 30 × 40 cm (12 × 16 inch) sheet cake pan with baking parchment. Grease lightly.

Beat the egg whites until stiff. Gradually add the sugar, beating until glossy. Combine the nuts, flour and cocoa and carefully fold into the egg whites.

Pour into the pan, spreading the batter with a spatula. Sprinkle with sliced almonds.

Bake in the center of the oven for 15–20 minutes.

Turn the cake out onto parchment paper sprinkled with sugar. Cover with the pan and let cool. Carefully remove the paper from the cake.

Whip the cream for the filling. Drain the mandarin oranges very well and fold them into the cream.

Spread the filling over the cake. Roll up from one long side, quite loosely, being careful not to let the cake crack. Sprinkle with powdered sugar.

PINOCCHIO TORTE *12 servings*

This sponge and meringue cake has many names and variations, including Mama's Meringue Torte and Glöminge Torte.

■ *Oven temp: 175 °C (350 °F), convection 175 °C (350 °F)*

75 g (5 tablespoons) butter, softened
2 dl (¾ cup) sifted powdered sugar
5 egg yolks
1 ½ dl (⅔ cup) all-purpose flour
1 ½ teaspoons baking powder
4 tablespoons (¼ cup) milk

Meringue:
5 egg whites
2 dl (¾ cup) sugar
50 g (½ cup) sliced almonds

Filling:
3 dl (1 cup) whipping cream

▶ Line a 30 × 40 cm (12 × 16 inch) sheet cake pan with baking parchment. Grease well.

Beat the butter and sugar until light and fluffy. Add the egg yolks, one at a time, beating well after each. Combine the flour and baking powder and add with the milk. Pour into the prepared pan, spreading the batter with a spatula.

Beat the egg whites until stiff. Fold in the sugar and beat for a few more minutes. Spread the meringue, slightly unevenly, over the cake batter. Sprinkle with almonds.

Bake on the center oven rack until the meringue is golden and the cake is dry, around 20 minutes.

Let the cake cool slightly. Turn out, carefully remove the baking parchment and cut in half, either crosswise or lengthwise.

Whip the cream and spread it over the meringue on one half of the cake. Top with the other half, meringue side up. Cut with a sharp knife to serve.

PAVLOVA TORTE *8–9 servings*

- *Oven temp: 150°C (300°F), convection 150°C (300°F)*

Meringue base:

4 egg whites
1 teaspoon 12% vinegar concentrate (or regular vinegar)
2 dl (¾ cup) sugar
1 teaspoon cornstarch
1 teaspoon vanilla sugar or ½ teaspoon vanilla extract

Garnish:

3 dl (1 cup) whipping cream
around 5 dl (2 cups) strawberries, red currants, blueberries, mango, carambola or raspberries

▶ Grease a 26 cm (10 inch) springform pan. Place the egg whites in a dry, clean bowl. Beat until stiff. Add the vinegar.

Combine the sugar and cornstarch and fold into the whites with the vanilla. Do not stir too much. Pour into the prepared pan.

Bake on a lower oven rack for around 1¼ hours. Let cool completely. Carefully remove the sides of the pan, then loosen the bottom. Whip the cream until thick. Spread it over the meringue. Garnish with fruit and berries.

MOCHA TORTE *16 servings*

■ *Oven temp: 125°C (250°F),*
  convection 125°C (250°F)

Meringue:
6 egg whites (2 dl / ¾ cup) egg whites
3½ dl (1½ cups) sugar

Mocha cream:
250 g (1 cup) unsalted butter
1 dl (⅓ cup) sifted powdered sugar
3 egg yolks (pasteurised) or 3½ tablespoons
  egg substitute (refrigerated or defrosted)
1½ dl (⅔ cup) cold strong brewed coffee

Garnish:
50 g (½ cup) sliced almonds
instant coffee granules

▶ Draw three circles, each one 22 cm (9 inches) in diameter, on baking parchment, two on one sheet and two on the other. Grease and flour the circles and place on baking sheets.

Combine the egg whites and sugar in a large bowl. Place in a pan of boiling water (the bowl should just fit in the pan) and beat until the meringue is thick and stiff. Pipe or spread the meringue over the circles.

Place the sheets in the oven immediately, one in the center, the other on a lower rack. Switch places a couple times during baking. In a convection oven, the sheets should be evenly spaced, and they do not need to be moved during baking. Bake for around 1¼ hours.

Remove the meringues from the parchment. Keep dry.

Beat the butter and powdered sugar until light and fluffy. Add the egg yolks one at a time, beating well after each. Stir in the coffee.

Spread coffee cream on two meringue layers. Stack. Top with the third layer. Spread the remaining coffee cream over the top and sides of the cake. Pipe a latticework of coffee cream over the cake. Toast the almonds and sprinkle around the sides of the cake. Sift instant coffee over the cake.

Instead of piping the cream over the cake, you can also spread a thicker layer of cream and then make a pattern with a fork.

MOCHA PASTRIES *10 pastries*

■ *Oven temp. 125°C (250°F),*
  convection 125°C (250°F)

½ batch meringue, see Mocha Torte

Filling:
½ batch mocha cream, see Mocha Torte

Garnish:
50 g (½ cup) sliced almonds
5 green or red
  candied
  cherries

Draw 20 circles, each one 5 cm (2 inches) in diameter, on baking parchment. Grease the parchment and place on a baking sheet. Beat the eggs and sugar for the meringues. Spoon into a pastry bag with a plain tip, around 1 cm (⅜ inch) in diameter, or spoon into a plastic bag and cut off the tip to form a hole around 1 cm (⅜ inch) in diameter. Begin in the center of each circle and pipe in a close spiral so that the entire circle is filled with meringue.

Bake on the center oven rack for around 30 minutes, until the meringue is dry. Let cool on a rack.

Prepare the mocha cream.

Sandwich two meringues with mocha cream in between. Spread a layer of cream around the edge. Roll the meringue sandwich in sliced almonds. Pipe the remaining cream over the cakes with a star tip. Place a half cherry in the center.

SCHWARZWALD TORTE

12 servings

This torte should be assembled just before serving.

- *Oven temp: 175°C (350°F), convection 175°C (350°F)*
2 dl/130 g (¾ cup/4 ounces) hazelnuts
2½ dl (1 cup) sifted powdered sugar
4 egg whites

Filling:
5 dl (2 cups) whipping cream
2 teaspoons vanilla sugar or 1 teaspoon vanilla extract
¾ dl (⅓ cup) ground nuts

Garnish:
100 g (3 ounces) semi-sweet chocolate
1–2 tablespoons cocoa

Draw three circles, each one 23 cm (9 inch) in diameter, on baking parchment. Place two on one baking sheet, one on the other. Grease and flour the circles. Lightly toast the nuts in the oven. Rub off the skins with a towel. Grind the nuts and mix with the powdered sugar.

Beat the egg whites until stiff. Carefully fold into the nut mixture. Spread the mixture over the circles.

Bake on the center oven rack for around 10 minutes.

Let cool.

Melt the chocolate for the garnish, see page 122. Spread in a thin even layer over baking parchment and let harden. Cut into wide diagonal strips, then into diamonds.

Whip the cream for the filling and stir in the ground nuts and vanilla.

Layer the meringues with cream in between. Spread cream over the top of the cake. Arrange chocolate diamonds in the cream on top of the cake. Sift cocoa over.

MARIE THERESE TORTE *10 servings*

■ *Oven temp: 175°C (350°F), convection 175°C (350°F)*

¾ dl (⅓ cup) chopped nuts
250 g (9 ounces) almond paste
125 g (½ cup) butter or stick margarine, softened
3 eggs
2 tablespoons all-purpose flour
½ teaspoon baking powder
Filling and garnish:
2 gelatin sheets
2 dl (1 cup) whipping cream
1 tablespoon vanilla + Kirschwasser
or cognac + sugar
5 dl (2 cups) strawberries or raspberries
½ dl (3 tablespoons) water
½ dl (3 tablespoons) sugar
½ teaspoon citric or ascorbic acid

▶ Grease a 20 cm (8 inch) cake pan, preferably low with a ruffled edge.

Sprinkle the chopped nuts over the interior of the pan.

Grate the almond paste. Add the butter and beat until light and fluffy. Beat in the eggs, one at a time, beating well after each. Combine the flour and baking powder and add, mixing lightly. Spread the batter in the prepared pan.

Bake on a lower oven rack for around 25 minutes. Let cool for a few minutes, then remove from the pan. Let cool completely

Soak the gelatin in cold water for at least 5 minutes. Place in a small saucepan and melt. Let cool slightly. Whip the cream. Fold the melted gelatin into the cream with the vanilla or cognac mixtures. Spread in a thick layer over the cake. Refrigerate until set.

Cover the entire filling with berries.

Simmer the water and sugar until syrupy. Stir in the citric acid. Let cool. Carefully spoon over the berries to make them look shiny.

MALAKOFF TORTE *around 12 servings*

This torte originated in Vienna.

■ *Oven temp: 175°C (350°F), convection 175°C (350°F)*

Base and garnish:
4 eggs
2 egg yolks
2 teaspoons vanilla sugar or 1 teaspoon vanilla extract
2½ dl (1 cup) sifted powdered sugar
100 g (1 cup) ground almonds
1½ dl (⅔ cup) all-purpose flour
Filling:
8 gelatin sheets
4 egg yolks
1 dl (½ cup) sifted powdered sugar
5 dl (2 cups) milk
1 tablespoon vanilla sugar or 1½ teaspoons vanilla extract
½ dl (3 tablespoons) white rum
3 dl (1¼ cups) whipping cream
Garnish:
1½ dl (⅔ cup) whipping cream
candied red cherries
lemon verbena leaves

▶ Draw three circles, each one 22 cm (9 inch) in diameter, on baking parchment. Place two on one baking sheet, one on the other.

Marie Therese Torte

Beat the eggs, egg yolks, vanilla and powdered sugar until very light yellow and very thick. Fold in the almonds and flour, mixing well.

Spread just under ¼ of the batter over each circle. Make ladyfingers, 2 × 6 cm (1 × 2 ½ inches) each, from the remaining batter.

Bake both on the center oven shelf, the cake layers for 12 minutes, the cookies for 8. Let cool on a flat surface.

Soak the gelatin in cold water for around 10 minutes.

Whisk the egg yolks, powdered sugar and milk in a saucepan. Simmer over low heat, whisking constantly, until somewhat thickened. Remove from the heat and add the gelatin sheets, stirring until melted.

Refrigerate the cream. Stir in the vanilla and rum. Whip the cream and fold into the cold egg cream.

Cover a serving platter with wide strips of parchment paper. Place a cake layer in the center. Place the ring from a springform pan around the cake. Line the inside with a strip of parchment paper. Arrange the cookies around the exterior, flat-side in. Fill with a layer of cream. Cover with another cake layer. Repeat. Cover the top with cream.

Refrigerate for several hours. Carefully remove the metal ring and paper. Whip the cream and pipe around the exterior with a star tip. Garnish with candied cherry halves and lemon verbena leaves.

If the cookies keep falling down as you line the metal ring, you may want to add them after the cake is finished. Attach to the cake with whipped cream just before the cookies serving.

Malakoff Torte

SCHWARZWALD CHOCOLATE CHERRY CAKE 15–20 servings

■ *Oven temp: sugar cookie base 200°C (400°F), convection 175°C (350°F); chocolate sponges 175°C (350°F); convection 175°C (350°F)*

Butter cookie base:
100 g (7 tablespoons) butter
2 dl (¾ cup) all-purpose flour
2 teaspoons cocoa
¼ teaspoon baking powder
2 teaspoons vanilla sugar or 1 teaspoon vanilla extract

Chocolate sponges:
4 eggs
2 tablespoons hot water
1 ¼ dl (½ cup) sugar
2 teaspoons vanilla sugar or 1 teaspoon vanilla extract
1 ¼ dl (½ cup) all-purpose flour
2 ½ tablespoons potato starch or cornstarch
1 tablespoon cocoa
⅛ teaspoon cinnamon
½ teaspoon baking powder

Filling:
2 tins (400 g /14 ounces each) pitted black cherries or
750 g fresh black cherries + ½–1 dl (¼–½ cup) sugar
2 ½ dl (1 cup) cherry juice (from the cherries)
1 tablespoon potato starch or cornstarch
1 tablespoon sugar
4 gelatin sheets
6 dl (2 ½ cups) whipping cream

Garnish:
200 g (7 ounces) semi-sweet or bittersweet chocolate
25 g (2 tablespoons) coconut fat or 2 tablespoons vegetable oil

▶ Dice the butter and place in a food processor with the other ingredients and pulse until the dough starts to form a ball. Cover with plastic wrap and refrigerate for around 30 minutes.

Roll the dough into a round sheet, around 24 cm (10 inches) in diameter. Place in a springform pan. Prick the dough with a fork.

Bake on the center oven rack for 15–20 minutes. Remove from the pan immediately and let cool on a rack.

For the chocolate sponges, grease and flour a 24 cm (10 inch) round cake pan. Beat the eggs and the hot water for 1–2 minutes. Add the sugar and vanilla and beat until light yellow and very thick. Combine the dry ingredients and fold into the egg mixture. Pour into the prepared pan.

Bake on a lower oven rack for 25–30 minutes. Let cool slightly, then remove from the pan. Halve horizontally.

Drain the tinned cherries, reserving the juice. Pit the fresh cherries and place in a saucepan. Add the sugar and heat to boiling. Drain, reserving the juice.

Combine the cherry juice (mixed with water, if necessary) with the potato starch in a saucepan. Heat to boiling, stirring constantly. Add the cherries and sugar to taste. Let cool slightly, then refrigerate.

Soak the gelatin in cold water for at least 5 minutes. Whip the cream. Squeeze excess water from the gelatin and melt over low heat or in the microwave oven. Let cool slightly, then pour in a thin stream into the cream, stirring lightly to blend.

Place the cookie base on a platter. Cover with half the cherry cream. Top with ⅓ of the whipped cream. Top with a chocolate sponge layer. Cover with the remaining cherry cream and a little whipped cream. Top with the remaining chocolate sponge.

Cover the entire torte with whipped cream, mounding it on top.

Melt the chocolate with the coconut fat in a water bath. Pour in a thin layer over parchment paper. Let it set. Make small rolls of chocolate with a potato peeler or cheese plane. Arrange on the torte. Refrigerate until ready to serve.

KING OSCAR'S TORTE

12–15 servings

Named after Oscar II, King of Sweden from 1872 to 1907.

- *Oven temp: 200 °C (400 °F), convection 175 °C (350 °F)*

100 g (1 cup) ground almonds
1 ½ dl (⅔ cup) sugar
4 egg whites

Nougat:
¾ dl (⅓ cup) sugar
3 tablespoons chopped almonds

Egg cream:
4 egg yolks
2 dl (1 cup) whipping cream
1 dl (½ cup) sugar
50 g (3 tablespoons) butter, softened

▶ Draw two circles, each one 24 cm (10 inch) in diameter, on baking parchment. Grease and flour the circles and place on a baking sheet.

Combine the almonds and sugar. Beat the egg whites until stiff. Fold into the nut mixture. Spread the mixture over the circles.

Bake on the center oven rack for around 15 minutes.

Remove the layers from the paper and let them cool.

For the nougat, melt the sugar and almonds in a skillet. Let caramelize until light brown. Pour onto an oiled or greased baking sheet and let cool completely. Crush in a mortar.

Whisk all the ingredients together in a saucepan. Simmer, whisking constantly until thickened. Do not allow to boil or the egg yolks will scramble. Add a little boiling water if that starts to happen, or if the mixture starts to separate. Let cool.

Stir the nougat into the egg cream. Spread half over one meringue layer. Top with the second layer and spread with the remaining nougat cream.

SANS RIVAL *15 servings*

This torte can be made a few days ahead of time.

- *Oven temp: 175 °C (350 °F), convection 175 °C (350 °F)*

500 g (18 ounces) almond paste
4–5 egg whites
or 1 batch King Oscar batter

Nougat:
1 ½ dl (⅔ cup) sugar
¾ dl (⅓ cup) chopped almonds

Buttercream:
2 dl (¾ cup) water
2 tablespoons butter
2 tablespoons all-purpose flour
2 egg yolks
250 g (1 cup) butter, softened
1 dl (⅓ cup) sifted powdered sugar
1 teaspoon vanilla sugar or ½ teaspoon vanilla extract

Garnish:
100–150 g (3–5 ounces) marzipan
red or green food coloring (optional)
25 g (¼ cup) sliced almonds

King Oscar's Torte

▶ Draw three squares, each one 20 cm (8 inch) per side, on baking parchment. Place on baking sheets. Lightly grease and flour.

Coarsely grate the almond paste. Lightly beat the egg whites. Mix together. Or prepare the mixture for King Oscar's Torte. Spread the cake batter in a thin layer over the squares.

Bake on the center oven rack for around 15 minutes, until dry and light golden.

Transfer the layers to a rack and let them cool completely.

For the nougat, melt the sugar and almonds in a skillet. Let caramelize until light brown. Pour onto an oiled or greased baking sheet and let cool completely. Crush in a mortar.

Heat the water with the 2 tablespoons butter in a small saucepan to boiling. Whisk in the flour and beat until the cream no longer sticks to the sides of the pan. Remove from the heat and whisk in the egg yolks. Let cool.

Beat the butter and powdered sugar. Beat in the egg yolk mixture, mixing thoroughly. Add the vanilla and nougat.

Spread the cream over the cake layers. Stack. Spread the cream over the top and sides.

Tint the marzipan, if desired, and roll into a thin sheet. Cut it into 3 cm (1 ¼ inch) strips with a pastry wheel or knife. Place them around the torte and place a couple of strips diagonally over the top.

Lightly toast the almonds and sprinkle over the torte.

Sans Rival

BIRGITTA'S ALMOND TORTE

12–15 servings

■ *Oven temp: 175°C (350°F),*
convection 175°C (350°F)
500 g (18 ounces) almond paste
3 egg whites
Filling and garnish:
3 dl (1 cup) whipping cream
2 tablespoons sugar
1 tablespoon sifted cocoa
1 tablespoon crushed instant coffee granules
2 teaspoons cocoa

▶ Draw two circles, each one 24 cm (10 inch) in diameter, on baking parchment. Place on a baking sheet. Grease lightly.

Coarsely grate the almond paste and beat with the egg white until smooth. Spread over the circles.

Bake on the center oven rack for 10–15 minutes or until light golden and dry.

Cool completely, then remove the paper.

Whip the cream. Fold in the sugar, cocoa and coffee. Spread the cream over both layers. Stack. Make a pattern in the cream on the top layer. Sift over cocoa.

Refrigerate for at least two hours before serving.

FILLED CREAM PUFF WREATH

See page 147.

ZOLA TORTE

See page 140.

MAZARIN TORTE

See the recipe on page 131 and the picture on page 163.

Tips for deep-frying

2 **The right amount of oil.** Fill the pan with just enough oil. It's easier to manage, and the risk of it bubbling over is smaller.

Stainless is best. Use a stable, solid pan of the appropriate size. Always keep a lid nearby. If the oil ignites, cover with the lid to extinguish the flames.

3 **The right temperature.** Do not exceed 180°C (360°F) when deep-frying. If the oil begins to smoke, it's too hot.

Check the temperature with a thermometer, or do the "bread test". Place a cube of white bread in the hot oil. If it turns golden brown after around one minute, the temperature is correct.

Heat the rosette iron. Heat the rosette iron with the oil, so that the iron is heated through. Heat the iron between each pastry.

Drain off excess oil. Place the deep-fried food on a double layer of paper towels to absorb excess fat. Then dip in sugar.

ROSETTES *approx. 20 pastries*

1 large egg yolk
2 tablespoons sugar
2 dl (1 cup) half and half
2 dl (1 cup) all-purpose flour
Deep-frying:
vegetable oil
Garnish:
sugar

▶ Combine all the ingredients and beat until smooth. Pour into a bowl that is wider than the rosette iron.

Heat the oil to 180°C (360°F). Use a thermometer or do the "bread test", see page 178. Heat the rosette iron in the oil at the same time.

Remove the iron and let excess oil drip off. Dip in the batter. Hold over the deep-fryer to set the batter a little.

Deep-fry until golden, around 1 minute.

Loosen from the iron with a fork. Drain on paper towels.

Reheat the iron before frying the next rosette.

Dip the rosettes in sugar.

FINNISH ROSETTES *approx. 35*

In Finland, these pastries are called *tippaleivät* are traditionally served on May 1, preferably with mead.

1 teaspoon dry yeast
2 tablespoons lukewarm water
2 ½ dl (1 cup) milk
2 eggs
1 ½ teaspoons sugar
½ teaspoon salt
5 dl (2 cups) all-purpose flour
Deep-frying:
vegetable oil
Garnish:
powdered sugar

▶ Sprinkle the yeast over the water. Let soften for around 5 minutes.

Heat the milk to 45–50°C (115–120°F). Beat the eggs, sugar and salt. Add the liquid. Gradually beat in the flour, mixing well. Cover and let rise for around an hour.

Heat the oil to 180°C (360°F). Use a thermometer or do the "bread test", see page 178.

Spoon the mixture into a piping bag with a narrow plain tip or use a plastic bag and cut a small hole in one corner. Pipe narrow, slightly concentric rings into the oil.

Fry one or two at a time until golden. Drain on paper towels.

Sift powdered sugar over.

FRIED COOKIE TWISTS
40–50 cookies

50 g (3 tablespoons) stick margarine or
  butter
I egg
I egg yolk
½ dl (3 tablespoons) sifted confectioner's sugar
I tablespoon cognac
grated zest of ½ lemon
2½ dl (I cup) all-purpose flour
Deep-frying:
vegetable oil
Garnish:
sugar

▶ Melt the butter and let it cool.

Beat the egg, egg yolk and confectioner's sugar until light yellow and very thick. All the sugar crystals should be dissolved. Add the cognac, lemon zest and melted butter. Stir in the flour.

Cover and refrigerate overnight.

Roll into a 2–3 mm thin sheet. Cut into 2–3 cm (1 inch) wide and 10 cm (4 inch) long strips. Make a slit in the center of each strip. Pull one end through each center slit, twisting the dough.

Heat the oil to 180 °C (360 °F). Use a thermometer or do the "bread test", see page 178.

Fry a few at a time until golden brown, about 1 minute per side.

Drain on paper towels.

Dip in sugar to coat both sides.

MAMA'S DEEP-FRIED RINGS
40 pastries

I egg
I dl (⅓ cup) sugar
I dl (⅓ cup) milk
2 tablespoons stick margarine or butter
around 5 dl (2 cups) all-purpose flour
I ½ teaspoons baking powder
Deep-frying:
vegetable oil
Garnish:
sugar

▶ Beat the egg and sugar until light yellow and very thick. Add the milk. Melt the butter and stir into the batter. Combine most of the flour with the baking powder and fold into the egg mixture.

Turn the dough out onto a floured surface. Knead lightly with a little flour so they don't stick. Roll into narrow ropes. Cut into 20 cm (8 inch) pieces and form into rings.

Heat the oil to 180 °C (360 °F). Use a thermometer or do the "bread test", see page 178.

Fry a few rings at a time until golden brown, around 1 minute per side.

Drain well on paper towels.

Dip in sugar to coat both sides.

ANISE COMBS *around 60*

100 g (7 tablespoons) butter or margarine
2 ½ dl (1 cup) milk
25 g (1 ounce) fresh yeast or 1 tablespoon
  active dry yeast
1 egg
¾ dl (⅓ cup) sugar
⅛ teaspoon salt
1–1 ½ teaspoons crushed anise seed
7 ½–8 dl (3–3 ⅓ cups) all-purpose flour

Deep-frying:
vegetable oil

Garnish:
sugar

▶ Melt the butter in a saucepan. Add the milk and heat to 37 °C (100 °F). If using dry yeast, heat to 45 °C (115 °F). Crumble the yeast in a little of the liquid, stirring until dissolved. Add the remaining liquid along with the egg, sugar, salt and anise. Knead in the flour.

Divide the dough in half. Roll each half into a 12 × 40 cm (5 × 16 inch) sheet. Cut into 4 strips, each 3 cm (1 ¼ inches) wide. Cut each strip into 8 pieces, each 5 cm (2 inches) long. Make several notches in each. Let rise for a while.

Heat the oil to 180 °C (360 °F). Use a thermometer or do the "bread test".

Deep-fry a few combs at a time for a couple of minutes, until golden.

Drain on paper towels.

If serving immediately, dip in sugar to coat both sides. Otherwise, they can be reheated and then dipped in sugar later.

JELLY DOUGHNUTS *10–12 servings*

1 dl (½ cup) milk
25 g (1 ounce) fresh yeast or 1 tablespoon
  active dry yeast
4 ½ dl (2 cups) all-purpose flour
50 g (3 tablespoons) stick margarine or
  butter, softened
2 tablespoons sugar
1 egg
2 teaspoons ground cardamom

Filling: around ½ dl (3–4 tablespoons)
thick fruit puree

Deep-frying: vegetable oil

Garnish: sugar

▶ Heat the milk to 37 °C (100 °F). If using dry yeast, heat to 45 °C (115 °F). Crumble the yeast in the milk, stirring until dissolved. Add 3 dl (1 ¼ cups) of the flour.

Beat the butter with the sugar, egg and cardamom. Add the remaining flour, beating well. Add the yeast mixture, kneading lightly. Cover and let rise for 30 minutes.

Roll into a 1 cm (⅜ inch) sheet. Make 6 cm (2 ¼ inch) circular indentations on half the dough. Place a spoonful of fruit puree in the center of each indentation. Fold over the remaining dough and cut circles with a plain cutter where you can see the mounds of puree. Press the edges to seal.

Heat the oil to 180 °C (360 °F). Use a thermometer or do the "bread test", see page 178.

Deep-fry the doughnuts until golden. Drain on paper towels. Roll in sugar.

CHOCOLATE BALLS *approx. 30*

100 g (7 tablespoons) butter or margarine,
   softened
1 dl (½ cup) sugar
1 tablespoon vanilla sugar or 1 ½ teaspoons
   vanilla extract
2–3 tablespoons sifted cocoa
3 dl (1 ¼ cups) rolled oats
2–3 tablespoons cold strong coffee
Garnish: pearl sugar or flaked coconut

▶ Beat the butter, sugar and vanilla until
light and fluffy. Stir in the remaining ingredients. Form into small round balls. Roll in
pearl sugar or coconut. Refrigerate until
serving time. Refrigerate leftovers.
   Pictured on page 177.

ARRAK BALLS *approx. 20*

100 g (7 tablespoons) butter or margarine,
   softened
1 dl (⅓ cup) sifted powdered sugar
1 teaspoon vanilla sugar or ½ teaspoon vanilla extract
tablespoons sifted cocoa
around 3 dl (1 ¼ cups) cookie or cake crumbs
arrak extract or Swedish "Punsch" liqueur
   to taste
Garnish:
chocolate sprinkles
or chopped toasted
   almonds

▶ Beat the butter, sugar, vanilla and cocoa
until light and fluffy. Stir in the crumbs. Add
arrak extract to taste. Refrigerate for at least
30 minutes.
   Form into small round balls. Roll in
chocolate sprinkles or chopped nuts. Place in
small cups and refrigerate until serving time.
Refrigerate leftovers.

ARRAK ROLLS *15 pieces*

Also called Vacuum Cleaners.
1 batch Arrak Balls
Garnish:
250–300 g (8–10 ounces) marzipan
green food coloring (optional)
semi-sweet or bittersweet chocolate

▶ Prepare the Arrak Ball mixture. Roll into 5
cm (2 inch) pieces. Tint the marzipan if desired. Roll the marzipan into a thin sheet. Cut
into 5 cm (2 inch) wide strips. Cover each
piece of arrak mixture with marzipan. Melt
the chocolate. Dip both ends of the rolls in
melted chocolate. Refrigerate.
   Pictured on page 177.

CHOCOLATE CRUNCH TOPS
approx. 20 pieces

☆ This recipe won a prize in 1984.
50 g (3 tablespoons) butter or stick
   margarine
½ dl (3 tablespoons) sugar
2 tablespoons light corn syrup or molasses
1 tablespoon cocoa
½ dl (3 tablespoons) shredded coconut
½ dl (3 tablespoons) raisins
2 dl (1 cup) rice flakes or other cereal

▶ Grease a sheet of parchment paper.
   Melt the butter in a saucepan. Stir in the
sugar, syrup and cocoa, mixing well. Heat to
boiling and let bubble for a few minutes.
   Stir in the remaining ingredients.
   Drop spoonfuls of the mixture onto the
prepared paper.
   Refrigerate until serving time.

RADIO CAKE *approx. 20 servings*

There are many names for this cake – Icebox Cake, Cookie Cake and Cellar Cake – to name a few.

200–250 g (7–9 ounces) solid coconut fat
200 g (7 ounce) semi-sweet or bittersweet chocolate
2 eggs (pasteurised) or 6 tablespoons egg substitute (refrigerated or defrosted)
3 dl (1 ¼ cups) powdered sugar
around 25 plain butter cookies

▶ Melt the coconut fat and chocolate in a saucepan over low heat. Let it cool.

Beat the eggs and powdered sugar until light yellow and very thick. Carefully and slowly stir the lukewarm chocolate mixture into the batter.

Line a 1 ½ liter (6 cup) loaf pan with baking parchment or heavy-duty plastic wrap. Spread a layer of chocolate in the bottom, then a layer of cookies, repeating, ending with chocolate.

Refrigerate until hard, preferably overnight. Cut into thin slices and serve immediately. Refrigerate leftovers.

WAFERS *20–25 cookies*

125 g (½ cup) butter
2 eggs
1 ¼ dl (½ cup) sugar
2 dl (¾ cup) all-purpose flour

▶ Melt the butter.

Beat the eggs and sugar until light yellow and very thick. Add the butter and fold in the flour.

Heat a "krumkake" iron. Brush lightly with butter. Spread the batter thinly over the iron. Bake. Remove and let cool on a rack.

WAFER BOWLS

Immediately drape the baked wafer over the bottom of a coffee cup or glass. Fill with whipped cream and fruit or berries.

ROLLED WAFERS

Bake Wafers, but as soon as each wafer is baked, roll up around the handle of a wooden spoon.

Wafer Bowls

Rolled Wafers

Gluten-Free and Low on Sugar

Many people are unable to enjoy all the pleasures of the cake table, due to food intolerance or allergies of different kinds.

Gluten intolerance means that a person cannot digest flour that contains gluten. All grains contain gluten to a greater or lesser degree – wheat flour contains the most gluten.

Gluten-free flour mixes are available, but the texture of bread and cakes made from them is somewhat different, rather short and crumbly.

Cornstarch, potato starch, cornmeal, rice flour and buckwheat flour are gluten-free.

Many cakes and tortes based on almonds, nuts or coconut do not contain any flour at all. And meringues are naturally free of gluten.

Remember that cake pans and baking sheets should be coated with gluten-free flour. Potato fiber, coconut and millet flakes, to name just a few, also can be used. Baking parchment is also a good substitute, as it does not need to be greased and floured.

Diabetics are not supposed to eat too much sugar and fat. Even if cakes and other sweets are not part of the everyday diet, most people like to splurge a little on festive occasions. It is possible to exchange a sandwich for a sweet roll, a piece of cake or a couple of cookies, if they are baked with very little sugar.

Good to know: You can cut the amount of sugar in sweet yeast bread to ½ dl (3 tablespoons) per 5 dl (2 cups) liquid.

Pie crust dough and puff pastry do not contain any sugar at all, and butter cookie dough can be made with very little sugar. Cream puff pastry is also sugar-free.

It is difficult to make cakes without sugar. It is needed to add volume when beating eggs or butter.

Certain sweetening agents can be used instead of sugar, but they often turn bitter when heated. That's why it's a better idea to reduce the amount of sugar in a recipe rather than use artificial sweeteners.

Index

Almond Cookies

Jitterbugs

Milan Logs

Anise Stars

Oat Cookies

Frosted Carrot Muffins

Fried Cookie Twists

Almond Balls

Sara Bernhardts

Almond Muffins

Almond Lace Cookies

Folded Cookies